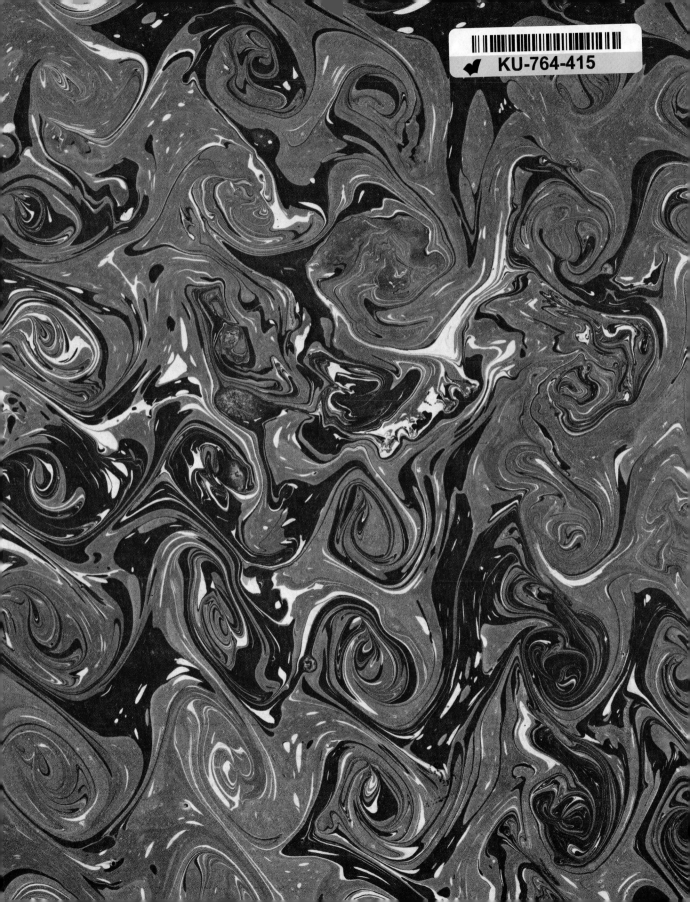

THE LION BOOK OF

CHRISTIAN CLASSICS

COMPILED BY VERONICA ZUNDEL

A LION BOOK
Tring · Belleville · Sydney

Copyright © 1985 Lion Publishing plc

Published by
Lion Publishing plc
Icknield Way, Tring, Herts, England
ISBN 0 85648 130 0
Albatross Books
PO Box 320, Sutherland, NSW 2232, Australia
ISBN 0 86760 607 X

First edition 1985

British Library Cataloguing in Publication Data

The Lion book of Christian classics.
  1. Christianity
  I. Zundel, Veronica
  200   BR121.2
  ISBN 0-85648-130-0

Printed and bound in Hong Kong by
Mandarin Offset International (HK) Ltd

Contents

Introduction

What makes a book a 'classic'? The number of editions published? The range of people it has spoken to? The fame of its author? Its historical interest as an example of a particular period? And does 'Christian classic' mean a work on spiritual matters or any product of a great Christian author's pen?

In some cases the questions are easy to answer. Augustine's *Confessions*, Thomas à Kempis' *Imitation of Christ*, Bunyan's *Pilgrim's Progress*—such books have earned the title 'classic' by many centuries of popularity and influence. Their success is due not only to a high quality of writing, but to the depth of spiritual experience which made such writing possible. The wisdom they contain is recognized even by those who would not share the author's Christian viewpoint.

But masterpieces rarely, if ever, appear out of nowhere. The greatest 'Christian classics' spring from times when the church was revitalized by new ways of understanding the truths of the Christian faith. Times such as the late Middle Ages, when both intellectuals and mystics made their own contributions to the knowledge and experience of God. Or the sixteenth and seventeenth centuries, with the powerful impetus of the Reformation followed by a renewal of personal devotion in the Roman Catholic church. Such periods naturally produced a wealth of literature. Behind the 'giants', the best-known works and authors, stand many others of lasting value and interest. In a small anthology one can only offer a taste of this rich banquet, and encourage the reader to explore further.

There are also works which, while not outstanding in themselves, have had an enormous effect on the thinking and lives of Christians. Books such as Brainerd's *Journal* or Carey's *Enquiry*, now largely unknown, deserve a place in the ranks of the classics because of their role in inspiring their readers to work and speak for God.

Sometimes 'Christian writing' has been too narrowly defined, as writing on theological subjects or for devotional purposes. But being a Christian is not just about 'religious' practices: prayer, Bible reading, church-going. It involves and affects our whole lives: our attitudes to others and to social structures, how we understand the world through philosophy and science, how we view and create art. So this collection is not only about the individual's relationship with God, but about many other areas of life.

No doubt if you introduced all the authors in this volume to each other, they would disagree strongly about many things. Some of them disagreed strongly in their lifetimes! Christians, even Christian writers, are not exempt from the human tendency to error. What they would all agree on, however, is that in Jesus Christ, God reached out to love and rescue sinners like themselves. It was in the name of Christ, God's Word made flesh, that they used words to enrich others. Whatever particular Christian tradition has nourished our own faith—or even if we are just beginning to seek faith—we can all be encouraged, challenged and inspired by their insights.

——————Veronica Zundel ——————

Early Christian Writings

FIRST TO THIRD CENTURIES

'If only we could get back to the purity of the early church!' Christians have often been heard to exclaim. But the church of the first few centuries had its own problems, as its writings show. With no tradition behind them, and at first not even an agreed New Testament, the generation which followed the apostles had to work out new patterns of worship and leadership, and decide how to live a Christian life in a pagan world, how to face persecution, how to maintain the unity of the church. Then there were doctrinal questions to be settled and wrong thinking to be corrected. The church leaders whom we know today as the Apostolic Fathers, and the theologians who followed them, have much to teach us as we grapple with similar questions today.

The Didache

FIRST OR SECOND CENTURY

Rediscovered in a Constantinople monastery in 1873, the *Didache*, or 'Teaching', may be the earliest piece of Christian literature outside the New Testament. It gives simple, practical instructions on Christian living and church organization.

THE FELLOWSHIP OF THE SPIRIT

By day and night, my son, remember him who speaks the word of God to you. Give him the honour you would give the Lord; for wherever the Lord's attributes are the subject of discourse, there the Lord is present. Frequent the company of the saints daily, so as to be edified by their conversation. Never encourage dissensions, but try to make peace between those who are at variance . . .

Do not be like those who reach out to take, but draw back when the time comes for giving . . . Give without hesitating and without grumbling, and you will see whose generosity will reward you. Never turn away the needy; share all your possessions with your brother, and do not claim that anything is your own. If you and he are joint participators in things immortal, how much more so in things that are mortal?

CLEMENT OF ROME

30?–100?

As bishop, or overseer, of the church in Rome, Clement
led his flock through severe persecution under the Emperor
Domitian. When prosperity returned, he was saddened to hear of
quarrels breaking out in the well-established Corinthian church.
His letter urging them to be reconciled became highly valued for its
teaching in all the churches.

—WHEN UNITY FOUNDERS—

Suppose there is friction and bad feeling in your church—what should you do, especially if you are involved in the arguments and divisions yourself? Further, let's suppose that you are in the right, that the trouble is not your fault, and that you are a mature and compassionate person. In that case, I suggest that you should say to the elders and members of the church: 'If I am in any way the cause of this trouble, even if unwittingly, or if my presence will in any way serve to perpetuate it, I will move to another congregation . . . I will go away anywhere you wish, and do anything the congregation says—anything, if it will contribute to peace among Christ's flock and its pastors.'

Anyone who adopts this attitude will deserve a high reputation amongst Christians, and God's approval.

—FROM '1 CLEMENT'—

JUSTIN

100?–165

After years of studying various philosophies Justin, a
pagan born in Samaria, accepted the Christian faith. From then on
he wrote vigorously in defence of the gospel, maintaining that
faith did not contradict reason. Eventually his activities led
to martyrdom.

—CHRISTIAN WORSHIP—

At the end of the prayers, we greet one another with a kiss. Then the president of the brethren is brought bread and a cup of wine mixed with water; and he takes them, and offers up praise and glory to the Father of the universe, through the name of the Son and of the Holy Ghost, and gives thanks at considerable length for our being

IGNATIUS OF ANTIOCH

35?–107?

The church in Antioch, where Jesus' followers were first called 'Christians', was torn apart by violent doctrinal controversies. Here Ignatius served as bishop and fought for the true faith. But it is as a martyr that he is most remembered. His courage and devotion to Jesus Christ shine out through the seven letters he wrote to different churches on his way to his death in Rome.

THROUGH DEATH TO CHRIST

All the way from Syria to Rome I have been chained to a detachment of soldiers who have behaved like animals towards me. I tried giving them money, but the more I gave them the more roughly they treated me. Quite honestly, they are like a pack of leopards, enjoying their role as hunters, with me as their prey. Well, that has some advantages. I may as well get used to 'leopards' now—it will be lions, and real ones at that, when I get to Rome. So I can make some progress towards preparing myself spiritually and mentally for what lies ahead. All I pray is that when the moment comes the lions will be quick about it . . .

Forgive me for writing like this, but I do know what is best for me. No power, human or spiritual, must hinder my coming to Jesus Christ. So whether the way be fire, or crucifixion, or wild beasts in the arena, or the mangling of my whole body, I can bear it, provided I am assured it is the way to him . . . So far as I am concerned, to die in Jesus Christ is better than to be king of the whole wide world! Do not try to tempt me to stay here by offering me the world and its attractions. Just let me make my way upward to that pure and undiluted light. For only when I get there will I truly be a man.

FROM 'LETTER TO THE CHURCH AT ROME'

---

counted worthy to receive these things at his hands. When he has concluded the prayers and thanksgivings, all the people present express their joyful assent by saying 'Amen' ('Amen' means 'so be it' in Hebrew) . . .

Then those whom we call deacons give to each of those present the bread and wine mixed with water over which the thanksgiving was pronounced, and carry away a portion to those who are absent.

We call this food 'Eucharist', which no one is allowed to share unless he or she believes that the things which we teach are true, and has been washed with the washing that is for remission of sins and unto a second birth, and is living as Christ commanded . . . For the apostles, in the memoirs called Gospels composed by them, have thus delivered unto us what was enjoined upon them: that Jesus took bread, and when he had given thanks, said, 'This do in remembrance of me, this is my body'; and that, in a similar way, having taken the cup and given thanks, he said, 'This is my blood'; and gave it to them alone.

FROM THE 'FIRST APOLOGY'

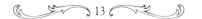

THE LETTER TO DIOGNETUS

150?

Like the Gospel-writer Luke, the unknown author of the
letter to 'Diognetus' wrote to explain the Christian faith
to a serious enquirer. Its recipient was probably a pagan of high
rank, possibly the emperor himself.

The first Christian centuries were a time of
great controversy, and debate as heresies threatened
the faith. This carving of a philosophical discussion
is from a second-century Christian sarcophagus.

CHRISTIANS IN THE WORLD

You can't tell a Christian from a non-Christian by where he lives or the way he speaks or how he dresses. There are no 'Christian towns', there is no 'Christian language', and they eat, drink and sleep just like everybody else. Christians aren't particularly clever or ingenious and they haven't mastered some complicated formula, like the followers of some religions.

But while it's true that they live in cities next to other people, and follow the same pattern of life as they do, in fact they have a unique citizenship of their own. They are,

of course, citizens of their own lands—loyal ones, too. But yet they feel like visitors. Every foreign country is their homeland, and their homeland is like a foreign country to them . . . They are nationals of various states, but citizens of heaven.

To put it simply—the soul is to the body as Christians are to the world. The soul is spread through all parts of the body and Christians through all parts of the world. The soul is in the body but is not of the body; Christians are in the world but not of the world.

IRENAEUS

130?–202?

One of the greatest threats to the Christian faith in its
early centuries was 'gnosticism', a philosophy based on so-called
'secret knowledge'. Irenaeus, a native of Asia Minor who became
a bishop in Gaul (modern France), reasserted the historic doctrines
of Scripture against this heresy.

WHAT CAN WE GIVE GOD?

God did not make the first man because he needed company, but because he wanted someone to whom he could show his generosity and love. God did not tell us to follow him because he needed our help but because he knew that serving him would make us whole. Our work for God—our service—adds nothing to his power or his achievements. He does not need anything we can give him, not even our obedience. But that does not mean that our work and service for him is meaningless or without value. God has promised to those who serve and follow him life, immortality and eternal glory. These rewards are specifically for servants who actually serve, and followers who actually follow.

FROM 'AGAINST HERESIES'

The Emperor Septimus Severus ruled from 193–211. Despite
opposition from the Roman government the church continued to
expand rapidly in the second and third centuries.

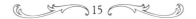

Tertullian

160?–220?

Tertullian was the first Christian author to write in
Latin, and so the first to use the word 'Trinity', and many other
'technical' words used later in theological debates. He was probably
converted to Christianity while practising law in Rome. Returning
to his native Carthage, in North Africa, he became a witty and
effective teacher of Christian doctrine.

GOD FROM GOD

When a ray is projected from the sun it is a
portion of the whole sun; but the sun will
be in the ray because it is a ray of the sun;
the substance is not separated but
extended. So from spirit comes spirit, and
God from God, as light is kindled from
light . . . This ray of God . . . glided down
into a virgin, in her womb was fashioned as
flesh, is born as man mixed with God. The
flesh was built up by the spirit, was
nourished, grew up, spoke, taught,
worked, and was Christ.

FROM 'APOLOGY'

While Tertullian was writing and lecturing in Carthage,
Alexandria, illustrated here on a Latin manuscript, was becoming
another important Christian centre. Christianity gained
respectability through the work of writers who explained the
faith in intellectual terms.

ORIGEN

185?–254?

Born into a Christian home, Origen became a brilliant biblical scholar and theologian. At the age of eighteen he was principal of a Christian school. In his great work, *On First Principles*, he sought to express Christianity in the terms used by Greek philosophy. Though later condemned by the church, he greatly influenced its thinking.

——THE SPIRIT'S WORK——

There would be no need for the Holy Spirit if we could become holy in our own strength, but God has sent him to our aid because we can't. We derive our existence from the Father; the Son, the 'Word', reveals the truth to our minds, and the Holy Spirit makes us holy. It is when the Holy Spirit has worked in us, making holy what was before unclean, that we can go on to receive God's righteousness in Christ . . . So the believer is intended to make progress, to grow. The Father gives natural life to everybody, but his purpose for us is so much more than that. He wishes us to go on to share more and more fully in Christ's righteousness, understanding and wisdom. Eventually—as the Holy Spirit cleanses and purifies us—all the stains of human sin and ignorance are removed and the being made by God becomes worthy of God. Then, and only then, is human destiny fulfilled.

Towards the end of his life Origen settled in Caesarea in Palestine. His fame as a writer and teacher soon made the town a rival of Alexandria.

EUSEBIUS

263?–339?

Eusebius developed his concern for thorough research under the influence of the brilliant biblical scholar Pamphilus, with whom he worked in the library at Caesarea. This, together with his deeply-held faith, led him to write his great work, the *History of the Church*. Compiled from hundreds of eye-witness records, it is largely a story of faith triumphing in the face of persecution. Eusebius himself had been imprisoned for his faith, witnessed many martyrdoms in Egypt, and in 310 saw his friend and mentor Pamphilus put to death. His work preserves many such stories of Christian heroism which would otherwise have been lost. 'If I can save from oblivion the successors not perhaps of all our Saviour's apostles but at least of the most distinguished,' he wrote in his introduction, 'I shall be content.'

———THE DEATH OF POLYCARP, BISHOP OF SMYRNA———

When the news spread round that it was Polycarp who had been captured, a deafening clamour broke out. He was brought before the governor, who asked if this was the man; and when Polycarp admitted it, tried to persuade him to recant. 'Have some respect for your years', he said; adding the rest of the usual exhortations, 'Swear an oath, "By the Luck of Caesar"; own yourself in the wrong and say, "Down with the infidels!"' Polycarp's brow darkened as he threw a look round the turbulent crowd . . . and then, indicating them with a sweep of his hand, he said with a growl and a glance to heaven, 'Down with the infidels!'.

The governor, however, still went on pressing him. 'Take the oath and I will let you go', he told him. 'Revile your Christ.' Polycarp's reply was, 'Eighty and six years have I served him, and he has done me no wrong. How then can I blaspheme my King and my Saviour?'

Persisting in his attempts, the governor then said again, 'Swear by the Luck of Caesar.' He answered, 'If you still think I am going to swear by Caesar's Luck, and still pretend not to know what I am, let me tell you plainly now that I am a Christian' . . .

The governor then said, 'I have wild beasts here. Unless you change your mind, I shall have you thrown to them.' 'Why then, call them up', said Polycarp, 'for it is out of the question for us to exchange a good way of thinking for a bad one . . .'

It was the governor who, on his part, now found himself completely at a loss. What he did next was to send his crier out to give out three times, from the centre of the arena, 'Polycarp has admitted to being a Christian!' At the crier's words the whole

Polycarp was one of many Christian martyrs whose courage in facing death bore witness to the reality of their faith and strengthened the church.

audience . . . broke into loud yells of ungovernable fury . . . they decided to set up a unanimous outcry that he should have Polycarp burnt alive.

It was all done in less time than it takes to tell. In a moment the crowd had collected faggots and kindling from the workshops and baths . . . the irons with which the pyre was equipped were fastened round him; but when they proposed to nail him as well, he said, 'Let me be; he who gives me strength to endure the flames will give me strength not to flinch at the stake, without your making sure of it with nails.' Then he cast his eyes up to heaven and said:

'O Lord God Almighty, Father of thy blessed and beloved Son Jesus Christ, through whom we have been given knowledge of thyself . . . I bless thee for granting me this day and hour, that I may be numbered amongst the martyrs, to share the cup of thine Anointed and to rise again unto life everlasting . . .'

As the amen soared up and the prayer ended, the men at the fire set their lights to it, and a great sheet of flame blazed out.

JOHN CHRYSOSTOM

350?–407

Known as the greatest of all Christian preachers, John cherished a youthful ambition to be a hermit. He was dissuaded by his Christian mother Anthusa, whose courage in facing widowhood at twenty occasioned the remark from John's non-Christian tutor, 'God, what women these Christians have!' After her death he ruined his health by living for several years in a mountain cave; but eventually he gave in to God's call, went back to Antioch and was ordained. His eloquence, his emphasis on 'the plain meaning of Scripture' (in contrast to the elaborate allegorical interpretation practised in Alexandria) and his love for his congregation led to his rapid rise as a popular preacher. He even had to ask people not to applaud during his sermons!

Against his will, John was made bishop of Constantinople. But his frequent references to politics, especially his attacks from the pulpit on the Empress Eudoxia, brought him into conflict with the government. When the empress deposed him, the people rioted and forced her to reinstate him. However, John refused to toe the line and in the end he was exiled for life. After his death he was given the title 'Chrysostom', or 'golden-mouthed'. 'Preaching makes me well', he once said. 'As soon as I open my mouth to speak, all my weariness is gone.'

WHY YOU NEED THE BIBLE

My usual custom is to let you know beforehand what subject I intend to preach on next week, so that before you come to church again you can read the passage for yourselves and get an idea of what it is all about. At the same time this will help you to remember what I have already said about the subject, and what still needs explaining; and so you will be better prepared to hear what I'm going to say next. And may I urge you—as I always have done, and always will—don't just listen carefully to what the preacher says, but take time regularly to read the Bible at home as well. This is something I never stop drumming into my friends and acquaintances!

Don't let anyone make excuses like these: 'I'm too busy with politics', 'I've got this or that public duty to fulfil', 'I'm a skilled worker, I must get on with my job', 'I've a wife and children to feed, I must provide for my family'; in other words, 'I'm a layman, it's not my business to read the Bible, I'll leave that to professional Christians like monks, nuns, priests and theology students.'

What on earth are you saying? It's 'not your business to read the Bible' because you've got too many other things to bother about? But that's the very reason why you need to read the Bible! The more worries you have, the more you need the Bible to keep you going! People like monks and nuns who have left the troubles of the world behind are quite safe; they are like ships sailing on a calm sea, or moored in a quiet harbour. But you are in the middle of

this godless world's stormy sea, and so you need spiritual help and sustenance far more urgently. They live far from the battlefield, out of the sound of gunfire; but you are in the front line, face to face with the enemy, and you are bound to suffer frequent blows and be severely wounded. So you need the medicine-chest close at hand.

Your wife irritates you, you worry about your children, your enemies are waiting to catch you out, someone you thought was your friend is jealous of you, your neighbour spreads rumours about you or picks quarrels with you, your colleague acts behind your back, someone sues you, you suffer from poverty, you lose your nearest and dearest, success gives you a boost and then trouble brings you down to

the depths again . . . Where can you find a suit of armour, or a castle from which to defend yourself? Where can you find ointment for your wounds, but in the Bible? . . .

Haven't you noticed how a smith, mason or carpenter, or any other craftsman, however much his back is against the wall, will never sell or pawn the tools of his trade? If he did, how could he earn his living? That is how we should think of the Bible; just as mallets, hammers, saws, chisels, axes and hatchets are the tools of the craftsman's trade, so the books of the prophets and the apostles, and all scripture inspired by the Holy Spirit, are the tools of our salvation.

FROM THE SERMON 'ON LAZARUS'

AUGUSTINE OF HIPPO

354–430

'Make me chaste, Lord, but not yet' is one of Augustine's most famous sayings. And 'not yet' was the keynote of his spiritual search for many years. Brought up in the Christian faith by his mother, Monica, he delayed his baptism and turned to the study of other philosophies. Manicheism, a belief that the world was created by a power of evil opposed to God, attracted him particularly.

But Monica continued to pray earnestly, and was assured by a Christian friend that 'the child of so many tears could not perish'. When Augustine's career as a teacher of rhetoric took him to Milan, he met the saintly Bishop Ambrose, and under his influence finally became a Christian. Only a few years later he himself was appointed bishop of Hippo, in his native North Africa. Here he wrote his *Confessions*, the model for all later autobiographies. And, as he saw the Roman Empire disintegrate around him, he felt compelled to write the highly influential *City of God*, which describes the relationship of the Kingdom of God to earthly kingdoms.

AUGUSTINE'S CONVERSION

There was a small garden attached to the house where we lodged . . . I now found myself driven by the tumult in my breast to take refuge in this garden, where no one could interrupt that fierce struggle in which I was my own contestant, until it came to its conclusion.

I probed the hidden depths of my soul and wrung its pitiful secrets from it, and when I gathered them all before the eyes of my heart, a great storm broke within me, bringing with it a great deluge of tears . . . For I felt that I was still enslaved by my sins, and in my misery I kept crying, 'How long shall I go on saying "Tomorrow, tomorrow"? Why not now? Why not make an end of my ugly sins this moment?'

I was asking myself these questions, weeping all the while with the most bitter sorrow in my heart, when all at once I heard the sing-song voice of a child in a nearby house. Whether it was the voice of a boy or a girl I cannot say, but again and again it repeated the chorus, 'Take it and read, take it and read'. At this I looked up, thinking hard whether there was any kind of game in which children used to chant words like these, but I could not remember ever hearing them before. I stemmed my flood of tears and stood up, telling myself that this could only be God's command to open my book of Scripture and read the first passage on which my eyes should fall . . .

So I hurried back to the place where Alypius was sitting, for when I stood up to move away I had put down the book containing Paul's letters. I seized it and opened it, and in silence I read the first passage on which my eyes fell: 'No orgies or drunkenness, no immorality or indecency, no fighting or jealousy. Take up the weapons of the Lord Jesus Christ; and stop giving attention to your sinful nature, to satisfy its desires.' I had no wish to read more and no need to do so. For in an instant, as I came to the end of the sentence, it was as though the light of faith flooded into my heart and all the darkness of doubt was dispelled.

———————— FROM 'CONFESSIONS' ————————

———THE TWO CITIES———

Though there are very many and great nations all over the earth, whose rites and customs, speech, arms, and dress, are distinguished by marked differences, yet there are no more than two kinds of human society, which we may justly call two cities, according to the language of our Scriptures. The one consists of those who wish to live after the flesh, the other of those who wish to live after the spirit . . .

Thus the things necessary for this mortal life are used by both kinds of men and families alike, but each has its own and widely different aim in using them. The earthly city, which does not live by faith, seeks an earthly peace, and the end it proposes, in the well-ordered concord of civic obedience and rule, is the combination of men's wills to attain the things which are helpful to this life. The heavenly city, or rather the part of it which sojourns on earth and lives by faith, makes use of this peace only because it must, until this mortal condition which necessitates it shall pass away.

————— FROM 'THE CITY OF GOD' —————

——— LATE HAVE I LOVED ———

Late have I loved you, O Beauty so ancient and so new; late have I loved you! You were within me, and I was outside; and I sought you outside and in my loneliness fell upon those lovely things that you have made. You were with me, but I was not with you. I was kept from you by those things, yet had they not been in you, they would not have been at all. You called me and cried to me and broke open my deafness; you sent forth your beams and shone upon me and chased away my blindness; you breathed your fragrance upon me, and I drew in my breath and now I pant for you; I tasted you, and now I hunger and thirst for you; you touched me, and I burn for your peace.

————— FROM 'CONFESSIONS' —————

DESERT FATHERS
FOURTH AND FIFTH CENTURIES

In 313 the Emperor Constantine, after his dramatic conversion, made Christianity the official religion of the Roman Empire. Church and state, until then often in violent conflict, became allies. Acceptance by 'the establishment' brought the church spiritual losses as well as material gains. Some Christians, reacting against the increasing 'worldliness' of the church, began to retreat to remote areas of Egypt and Syria to live a more demanding Christian life. Singly or in groups, they spent their time in prayer, Bible reading and fasting. People came from great distances to seek their advice on spiritual matters.

The most famous hermit of all was Antony. Around him, as around many of the more extreme hermits, fanciful stories of strange visions and miracles grew up. But the authentic sayings of the 'desert fathers', collected by their followers, are witty, down-to-earth and full of practical wisdom.

At the foot of Mt Sinai stands St Catherine's monastery, one of the oldest monasteries in the world.

—MARY NEEDS MARTHA—

A certain brother came to Abbot Silvanus at Mount Sinai, and seeing the hermits at work he exclaimed: 'Why do you work for the bread that perishes? Mary has chosen the best part, namely to sit at the feet of the Lord without working.' Then the abbot said to his disciple Zachary: 'Give the brother a book and let him read, and put him in an empty cell.' At the ninth hour the brother who was reading began to look out to see if the abbot was not going to call him to dinner, and some time after the ninth hour he went himself to the abbot and said, 'Did the brethren not eat today, Father?' 'Oh yes, certainly', said the abbot, 'they have just had dinner'. 'Well', said the brother, 'why did you not call me?' 'You are a spiritual man', said the elder, 'you don't need this food that perishes. We have to work, but you have chosen the best part. You read all day, and can get along without food.' Hearing this the brother said, 'Forgive me, Father.' And the elder said, 'Martha is necessary to Mary, for it was because Martha worked that Mary was able to be praised.'

BENEDICT OF NURSIA

480?–547?

'We propose . . . to establish a school of the Lord's
service' says Benedict in the introduction to his *Rule*. Benedict's was
not the first 'school' of this kind. There had been monks since the
early fourth century, when hermits in the Egyptian desert began to
live together under a common discipline, and Basil the Great had
written a rule which is still used in Eastern monasteries today. But Benedict's
Rule gradually superseded all other rules used in Western monasteries.

Since the time of Benedict there
has been a monastic community
at Monte Cassino in Italy.

Benedict himself, like the earliest monks, started as a
hermit, living in the hill country of Subiaco, near Rome. Disciples
soon gathered around him, and he established twelve small
communities. In 530 he fled from persecution to Monte Cassino,
between Rome and Naples, where he became abbot of a large and
flourishing community.

His monks lived a simple and austere life, gathering for
prayers seven times a day, and spending the rest of their time in
manual work (everyone took a turn in the kitchens!), private prayer
and study. Great care was taken of the sick, the elderly, guests and
erring brothers. It is this compassion, wisdom and moderation in
Benedict's instructions which account for the *Rule*'s appeal and its
continued popularity today.

REACHING A COMMON MIND

Whenever anything important has to be done in the monastery the abbot must assemble the whole community and explain what is under consideration. When he has heard the counsel of the brethren, he should give it consideration and then take what seems to him the best course. The reason why we say that all should be called to council is this: it is often to a younger brother that the Lord reveals the best course. But the brethren must give their counsel submissively and humbly and not presume stubbornly to defend their opinions.

THE COMMUNITY AT WORSHIP

As the prophet puts it, 'Seven times daily I have praised you.' This sacred number of seven will be performed by us if we carry out the duties of our service at Lauds, Prime, Terce, Sext, None, Vespers and Compline . . . Let us therefore at these times give praise to our Creator . . . and at night let us get up to thank him.

We believe that God is present everywhere, and that the eyes of the Lord are in every place, keeping watch on the good and the bad . . . We must therefore consider how we should behave in the sight of the Divine Majesty, and as we sing our psalms let us see to it that our mind is in harmony with our voice.

HOSPITALITY

All who arrive as guests are to be welcomed like Christ, for he is going to say, 'I was a stranger and you welcomed me.' Special care is to be shown in the reception of the poor and of pilgrims, for in them especially is Christ received; for the awe felt for the wealthy imposes respect enough of itself.

WHEN BROTHERS FALL

The abbot should carry out with the deepest concern his responsibility for the brethren who fall into sin, 'for it is not those who are in good health who need a doctor, but those who are sick'. For this reason he should, like a skilful doctor, use every possible remedy; for example, he may send . . . mature and wise brethren to give unofficial consolation to their wavering brother . . . 'so that he is not overcome by too much sadness'. And so let it be as the apostle also says, 'that love is reaffirmed towards him'; and everybody is to pray for him.

DAILY NEEDS

No one may take it upon himself to give or receive anything without the abbot's permission or to possess anything as his own, anything whatever, books or writing tablets or pen or anything at all . . . Everything should be common to all . . .

We consider it to be enough for the daily meal . . . that there should always be served two cooked dishes, to allow for the weaknesses of different eaters; so that if someone cannot eat of the one dish he may still make a meal from the other . . .

If, however, their work is rather heavy, it will be in the abbot's power . . . to decide whether it is expedient to increase the allowance. But there must be no danger of overeating, so that no monk is overtaken by indigestion, for there is nothing so opposed to Christian life as overeating . . .

Clothing should be given to the brethren according to the nature of the district where they live and the climate . . . Those who receive new clothes should always give the old ones back at once; they can be stored in the wardrobe for the benefit of the poor. For it is sufficient for a monk to have two tunics and two cowls, to allow for wear at night and for washing; more than that is superfluous, and should be taken away.

ANSELM
1033–1109

'At the pressing entreaties of some of my brethren I published a short work as an example of meditation on the meaning of faith, from the point of view of someone . . . seeking to understand what he believes.' The book Anselm introduced with these words was *Proslogion*, and in it he included his famous 'ontological proof'—an attempt to prove by logic that God exists. It was this that earned him the title of 'father of scholasticism', the medieval system of study whereby scholars analysed their faith using the methods of classical philosophy.

A restless youth, Anselm ran away from his wealthy home in Lombardy to join the Abbey of Bec in Normandy. There he studied under Lanfranc and later succeeded him as abbot. After the Norman conquest of Britain, Anselm again followed Lanfranc, this time as Archbishop of Canterbury. Conflict with the monarchy led to two periods of exile, but each time Anselm was restored to office. He was a caring pastor who championed humanitarian causes such as the suppression of the slave trade. But it is for his writings—especially *Cur Deus Homo?* (Why Did God Become Man?)—that he is justly revered.

THE REALITY OF GOD

Now, Lord, since you are the one who adds understanding to faith, help me to understand (as far as you think fit) that you do exist, as we believe, and that you are what we believe you to be. We believe that you are the greatest thing imaginable . . . And it is certain that this 'greatest thing imaginable' cannot exist only in the mind. For if it exists only in the mind, we can imagine it existing in reality too—but that would be something greater! . . .

So there can be no doubt at all that this 'greatest thing imaginable' does exist both in the mind and in reality. Its existence is so real, that it is impossible to imagine it *not* existing . . . It is yourself, our Lord and God . . . For everything except yourself can be imagined as non-existent. You alone most truly exist; you are more completely real than anything else . . . You fill and embrace all things, you exist before and

beyond all things . . . Lord, you alone are what you are and who you are . . .

> My God,
> I pray that I may so know you and
>   love you
> that I may rejoice in you.
> And if I may not do so fully in this
>   life
> let me go steadily on
> to the day when I come to that
>   fullness . . .
> Meanwhile let my mind meditate
>   on it
> let my tongue speak of it
> let my heart love it
> let my mouth preach it
> let my soul hunger for it
> my flesh thirst for it
> and my whole being desire it
> until I enter into the joy of my Lord.

FROM 'PROSLOGION'

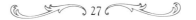

BERNARD OF CLAIRVAUX

1090–1153

In the 'Dark Ages', the monasteries alone kept the flame
of learning alight in Europe. But in the process they lost the
simplicity of life outlined in Benedict's *Rule*. In 1097 the monks of
Citeaux in Burgundy decided to follow a much stricter way of life.
They did away with servants and personal possessions, ate frugally
and lit a fire only once a year.
At first the severity of the Cistercian rule attracted few
new members. Then in 1112 Bernard, a young nobleman from
Dijon, arrived. His enthusiasm for the monastic life was so
catching that soon thirty of his friends and relations had joined up.
It is said that women hid their sons and husbands when
he came 'recruiting'!
In 1115 Bernard founded a daughter house at Clairvaux.
Though his desire was for a secluded life, his great abilities soon
involved him in the politics of church and state, and he even
influenced the election of a new pope. Bernard's personal life was
one of extreme self-denial, but his writings—*On the Song of Songs*
and *On the Love of God*—constantly emphasize that God is love and
can be found only by love.

THE POVERTY OF RICHES

It is natural for a rational being always to seek those things which, in his judgment, are better and more useful for his ends; and he is never satisfied until he has acquired the thing that he prefers. A man who has a pretty wife, for instance, looks round with roving eye to find a fairer woman; if he has got a costly suit of clothes, he wants one even better; however rich he is, he will be jealous of anyone who is more wealthy still. You see it happening every day: land-owners still 'lay field to field' . . . and those who live in spacious palaces and royal habitations are daily joining house to house and ever in a fever building new or taking down and altering the old—rectangular for round or round for square. And men in high position, too, are they not always on the climb, trying to hoist themselves to higher places still? There is no limit to such restlessness, because in all these things the absolute can never be attained. It is on this endless treadmill that the ungodly walk . . . Suppose you saw a starving man inhaling great deep breaths, filling his cheeks to stay his hunger, would you not call him mad? And it is just as mad to think that blowing yourself out with earthly goods can satisfy your reasonable soul.

FROM 'ON THE LOVE OF GOD'

Bernard of Clairvaux stressed the importance
of personal devotion. This detail from
a thirteenth-century window in Canterbury
Cathedral, England, is of two monks praying.

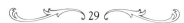

FRANCIS OF ASSISI

1182–1226

Every day, thousands of visitors from all over the world
flock to the tiny hill town of Assisi in northern Italy to see the
home of 'everyone's favourite saint'. The story of how Francis,
playboy son of a wealthy cloth merchant, became 'Il Poverello', the
'little poor one', has captured the popular imagination for centuries.

All of Francis' actions were dramatic. When, inspired by
a vision, he renounced his riches, he did so in the market square by
stripping off his clothes and returning them to his father. When he
heard the call to serve Christ by serving the poor, he started by
kissing a leper. When he went out to preach, the story goes that he
preached not only to people but also to the birds and even to a
wolf. When his childhood friend Clare was prevented by her
parents from embracing poverty as Francis had done, Francis
arranged her kidnapping.

His simplicity and joy were infectious. By the time
'Brother Ass', as he called his body, submitted to 'Sister Death', his
followers were numbered in thousands. Legend and fact are
intertwined in the biographies which soon abounded. What is
certain is that the command to 'rebuild my church', which Francis
heard while young in the ruined church of San Damiano and at
first took literally, was fulfilled by this remarkable man who took
'Lady Poverty' for his bride.

One day they arrived in a town famished, and in accordance with the Rule, went to beg bread for the love of God, Saint Francis going along one street and Brother Masseo along another. But because Saint Francis was undistinguished in appearance and short of stature, and was therefore considered a poor, miserable little man by those who did not know him, he collected nothing but a few morsels and crusts of dry bread. But Brother Masseo, who was a tall and handsome man, was given good large pieces and even whole loaves.

When they had ended begging, they met again outside the town to eat at a place where there was a beautiful spring, and beside it a fine broad rock, on which each laid the alms he had received. And when Saint Francis saw that the pieces of bread obtained by Brother Masseo were far better and larger than his own, he was filled with great joy, and said, 'O Brother Masseo, we are not worthy of so great a treasure!' And when he had repeated these words many times, Brother Masseo replied, 'Dearest father, how can one call this treasure, when we are so poor, and lack so many things that we need? We have no cloth, no knife, no dish, no bowl, no house, no table, and no man or woman to wait on us.'

Then Saint Francis answered: 'And that is what I call a great treasure, where nothing has been provided by human labour, but everything has been given by divine Providence, as we can see clearly in the bread that we have collected, in this fair table of stone, and in this spring of clear water. So I would have us pray God that he will cause us to love with all our hearts this treasure of Holy Poverty who is so noble that God himself is her servant.'

FROM 'THE LITTLE FLOWERS OF ST FRANCIS'

THE WAY TO HUMILITY

A servant of God cannot know the extent of his patience and humility so long as all goes well with him. But when a time comes that those who should treat him well do the opposite, then he shows the true extent of his patience and humility, and no more.

Blessed is the servant who does not esteem himself as better when he is praised and promoted by men than when they look on him as vile, stupid and contemptible; for whatever a man is in the sight of God, that he is, and no more.

Blessed is the servant who accepts rebuke with courtesy, obeys respectfully, confesses humbly, and makes amends gladly. Blessed is the servant who is not in a hurry to excuse himself, but humbly accepts shame and reproach for a fault even when he is not to blame.

> Where there is charity and wisdom,
>   there is neither fear nor ignorance.
> Where there is patience and humility,
>   there is neither anger nor vexation.
> Where there is poverty with joy,
>   there is neither greed nor avarice.
> Where there is peace and meditation,
>   there is neither anxiety nor doubt.
> Where the fear of the Lord stands
>   guard, there the enemy finds no
>   entry.
> Where there is mercy and
>   moderation, there is neither
>   indulgence nor harshness.

FROM 'THE COUNSELS'

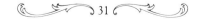

THOMAS AQUINAS
1225–1274

'To know Thomas is to know the medieval mind at its finest' says one modern critic. A plump, slow boy who was later to be nicknamed 'the dumb ox' by his fellow-students, Thomas was sent at five to the historic Abbey of Monte Cassino and at fourteen to the University of Naples.

Inspired by a lecturer, he resolved to join the Dominican order of friars. His wealthy family, who lived at nearby Aquino, responded by kidnapping him. His brothers tempted him with a prostitute (whereupon Thomas threw a burning log at them!) and an offer to buy him the position of Archbishop of Naples. But Thomas stood firm and went to Paris to study. There, and in Cologne, studying under Albert the Great, his brilliance soon became apparent. He was awarded a master's degree in theology at thirty-one, four years below the usual age; and he lectured both in Paris and Italy.

His writings fill eighteen volumes, the most famous being the *Summa Theologiae* and the *Summa Contra Gentiles* in which he attempted to set out a complete and systematic philosophical analysis of Christian doctrine. But after an overwhelming experience of God which came to him while celebrating mass in December 1272, he gave up writing, saying, 'Such things have been revealed to me that all I have written seems as so much straw.'

NEW WORDS FOR OLD TRUTHS

The word 'person' is not discovered in the text of the Old or New Testament as referring to God. Yet what this word means is often present in Holy Scripture, namely, that he is the peak of self-existence and most perfect in wisdom.

If we were restricted to speak of God only in the words used in Holy Scripture, it would follow that no one could speak of God in any other language than the one used in the Old and New Testaments. Because we must have dialogue with non-believers, it is necessary for us to discover new words about God expressing the ancient belief . . .

The truth of the faith is diffused throughout Holy Scripture in various ways, and sometimes obscurely. Hence, to bring out the truth of the faith from Holy Scripture requires long study and training. But not everyone who needs to know the truth of the faith can devote themselves to study. So a clear summary is needed of the truth set forth in Holy Scripture, so that everyone has the opportunity to believe it. This summary is not an addition to Holy Scripture; rather, it is drawn from Holy Scripture.

FROM 'SUMMA THEOLOGIAE'

Aquinas' reputation as a philosopher and theologian spread throughout medieval Europe. The Priors' Palace in Perugia, central Italy, dates from the end of the thirteenth century.

WAYS OF PROVING GOD

God's existence can be proved in five ways. First and most obvious is the way that begins with change. It is obvious that some things in the world are undoubtedly in the process of changing. But anything undergoing change is being changed by something else . . . Moreover, if this something else is in the process of changing, it itself is being changed by another thing, and this by another. Now the changing has to stop somewhere, or else there will be no first cause of the changing . . . And so we have to come to some first cause of changing that is not itself changed by anything else, and this is what everyone understands by God.

The second way is derived from the nature of causation. In the physical world we find causes in an order of succession; we never see, nor could we, anything causing itself, for then it would have to pre-exist itself, and this is impossible . . . We must therefore suppose a First Cause, which all call 'God'.

The third way is drawn from the existence of the unnecessary and the necessary . . . Our experience includes things certainly capable of existing but apparently unnecessary, since they come and go, being born or dying. But if it is unnecessary for a thing to exist, it did not exist once upon a time—and yet everything cannot be like this, for if everything is unnecessary, there was once nothing. But if such were the case, there would now be nothing, because a non-existent thing can only be brought into existence by something already existing . . . Hence we are compelled to suppose something that exists necessarily, having this necessity only from itself; in fact, it itself is the cause why other things exist.

The fourth way is supported by the gradation noticed in things. There are some things that are better, more true, more noble, and so forth, and other things less so . . . There is therefore a truest and best and most noble thing, and so most fully existing . . . And this we call 'God'.

The fifth way is taken from the ordered tendencies of nature. All bodies which follow natural laws show a direction of actions to a goal, even when they are without awareness . . . Anything, however, without awareness, tends to a goal only under the guidance of someone who is aware and knows; the arrow, for instance, needs an archer. Everything in nature, consequently, is guided to its goal by someone with knowledge and this one we call 'God'.

FROM 'SUMMA THEOLOGIAE'

MEDIEVAL MYSTICS
THIRTEENTH AND FOURTEENTH CENTURIES

'It was not by his motions that he was recognized by me,
nor could I tell by any of my senses that he had penetrated to the
depths of my being . . . only by the movement of my heart.' Thus
Bernard of Clairvaux described an encounter with God which went
beyond sense or language. Such 'mystical' encounters have been the
common experience of Christians throughout the ages who
earnestly sought God.
Perhaps in reaction to the intellectualism of men such as
Bernard's arch-enemy Peter Abelard, who argued that truth could
be reached through reason alone, there was a remarkable outbreak
of mystical experience in the late Middle Ages. The men and
women, particularly in Britain and Germany, to whom these
revelations came, were eager to direct others through the joys and
dangers of contemplative prayer and meditation. The books they
wrote as a result are classic guides to the inner life of the believer.

MEISTER ECKHART
1260–1327

A promising student from a poor German village,
Johannes Eckhart was sent by the Dominican friars to Cologne and
Paris, where he gained a master's degree in theology. He soon rose
to high office in the Dominican order, and travelled throughout
Germany and France giving lectures. His rather eccentric teaching
brought him condemnation as a heretic, but his influence helped
renew the spiritual life of Germany.

—EMPTYING THE CASK—

No cask can hold two different kinds of drink. If it is to contain wine then they must of necessity pour the water out; the cask must become empty and free. Therefore, if you are to receive God's joy and God, you are obliged to pour out created things . . . In a few words, everything that is to receive and be capable of receiving should and must be empty . . .

Therefore, if you want to have and to find complete joy and consolation in God, make sure that you are naked of all created things, of all comfort from created things; for truly, so long as created things console you and can console you, never will you find true consolation. But when nothing but God can console you, then truly God does console you, and with him and in him everything that is joy consoles you.

FROM 'THE BOOK OF DIVINE CONSOLATION'

JAN VAN RUYSBROECK

1293–1381

At the age of eleven Jan ran away from his Flemish
village to join his uncle, a canon of Brussels Cathedral. Here he
eventually became a cathedral chaplain and campaigned vigorously
for the orthodox faith against a breakaway mystical group who
believed that man was divine and needed no laws. Described as a
quiet, shabby person who 'went about the streets of Brussels
with his mind lifted up into God', Jan left the city when he was fifty
to found a small community in the forest, living in constant prayer.

ON FALSE MYSTICS

Some unbelieving and perverse men . . .
say that they have no God, but that they
are so wholly dead to themselves, and
united with God, that they have themselves become God . . . These men have
gone astray into the vacant and blind
simplicity of their own being . . . and the
onefold simplicity which they there
possess, they take to be God, because they
find a natural rest therein . . . and, because
of the naked emptiness which they feel and
possess, they say that they are without
knowledge and without love, and are
exempt from the virtues. And so they
endeavour to live without heeding their
conscience . . . They would know and heed
as little of all the works which God has
wrought, and all that Scripture teaches, as
though not one line had ever been written;
for they believe themselves to have found
and to possess that for the sake of which all
Scriptures have been made, namely, the
blind essential rest which they feel. But in
fact they have lost God and all the ways
which may lead to him; for they have no
more inwardness, nor more devotion, nor
holy practices, than a dead beast has.

FROM 'THE BOOK OF SUPREME TRUTH'

JOHANN TAULER

1300?–1361

Like his contemporaries Eckhart and Suso, who
influenced him, Tauler was a Dominican friar and benefited from
the thorough education the Dominicans provided. His greatest
popularity was with the common people of the Rhineland, to whom
he preached in their own dialect. Perhaps the most practical of all
mystics, he uses in his sermons homely illustrations to make simple
but profound spiritual points.

ANCHORED IN GOD

The devil can bring us into all kinds of
trouble. 'Oh', people say, 'if only I had a
spiritual director to talk to! I get the most
fearful ideas, and I am in a dreadful state.'
Well, my dear child, I know a lot about the
ideas the devil can put in our minds, and
my advice is this—what the devil puts in
your mind, you put out again; be at peace

and turn your heart to God. Pay no attention to such ideas, do not let your thoughts dwell on them, just let them pass out of your mind. You will often suffer such painful experiences; this is the devil's doing, and it comes from inordinate melancholy. He will end by bringing you to despair. 'It is all no use', you will say.

What ought you to do then? Lay the burden of all your cares on God, anchor yourself in him. When sailors are in danger and think they are going to run aground on the rocks, they throw their anchor overboard and it sinks to the bottom of the Rhine, and that saves them. We should do the same; when the devil attacks us with dreadful temptations of mind or body, there is nothing for it but to throw our anchor overboard, the anchor of perfect trust and hope in God. Never mind about the oars and the rudder, the anchor is all you need; and this is what you must do in every distress of soul or body.

———————— FROM 'SPIRITUAL CONFERENCES' ————————

Johann Tauler's sermons, preached to the people of the Rhineland, explained the meaning of being a Christian in simple, practical terms.

HEINRICH SUSO

1300–1366

Heinrich, the son of a rich Swabian family, was
converted as a teenager and became a Dominican friar. He was
much criticized for his support of Meister Eckhart and because it
was said he mixed with women too freely; and eventually he was
exiled. But his writings, in 'simple language for simple folk',
remained immensely popular.

JULIAN OF NORWICH

BORN 1342?

As a young woman, Julian prayed for a serious illness to
help her understand the sufferings of Christ. At thirty the illness
came, and with it a series of sixteen 'showings', or visions.
For the rest of her life she lived as a hermit in a cell attached
to St Julian's church in Norwich, from which she took her name.
As she meditated on her visions and began to understand their
meaning, she wrote and rewrote her account of them, the
Revelations of Divine Love.

——— ALL THAT IS MADE ———

It was at this time that our Lord showed me
spiritually how intimately he loves us. I
saw that he is everything that we know to
be good and helpful. In his love he clothes
us, enfolds and embraces us; that tender
love completely surrounds us, never to
leave us . . .

And he showed me more, a little thing,
the size of a hazelnut, on the palm of my
hand, round like a ball. I looked at it
thoughtfully and wondered, 'What is this?'
And the answer came, 'It is all that is
made.' I marvelled that it continued to
exist and did not suddenly disintegrate; it
was so small. And again my mind supplied
the answer, 'It exists, both now and for
ever, because God loves it.'

——— THE MEANING ——— OF THE VISIONS

From the time when these things were first
revealed I had often wanted to know what
was our Lord's meaning. It was more than
fifteen years after that I was answered in my
spirit's understanding. 'You would know
our Lord's meaning in this thing? Know it
well. Love was his meaning. Who showed it
you? Love. What did he show you? Love.
Why did he show it? For love. Hold on to
this and you will know and understand
love more and more. But you will not know
or learn anything else—ever!

Eternal Wisdom: Now answer me a question, after all this searching for hidden things: what is it that, among all things, tastes best to the highest spirit?

The Servant: Alas Lord, I should like to know this from you; for the question is too high for me.

Wisdom: Then I will tell you. Nothing tastes better to the highest spirit than to fulfil my will in all things. And if he knew that my glory depended on rooting out nettles or other weeds, that would be to him the most desirable thing to accomplish.

The Servant: Ah Lord, how you strike at me with this question!

── FROM 'THE LITTLE BOOK OF ETERNAL WISDOM' ──

THE CLOUD OF UNKNOWING
1370?

'I do not mind at all if the loud-mouthed, or flatterers, or the mock-modest, or fault-finders, gossips, tittle-tattlers, talebearers, or any sort of grumbler, never see this book' writes its unknown author, 'I have never meant to write for them.' Instead he (possibly a country parson in the East Midlands of Britain) wrote for those 'really and wholly determined to follow Christ perfectly . . . to the utmost height of the contemplative life.'

── BY LOVE HE MAY BE CAUGHT ──

But now you will ask me, 'How am I to think of God himself, and what is he?' and I cannot answer you except to say, 'I do not know!' For with this question you have brought me into the same darkness, the same cloud of unknowing where I want you to be! For though we through the grace of God can know fully about all other matters, and think about them—yes, even the very works of God himself—yet of God himself can no man think. Therefore I will leave on one side everything I can think, and choose for my love that thing which I cannot think! Why? Because he may well be loved, but not thought. By love he can be caught and held, but by thinking never.

Therefore, though it may be good sometimes to think particularly about God's kindness and worth, and though it may be enlightening too, and a part of contemplation, yet in the work now before us it must be put down and covered with a cloud of forgetting. And you are to step over it resolutely and eagerly, with a devout and kindling love, and try to penetrate that darkness above you. Strike that thick cloud of unknowing with the sharp dart of longing love, and on no account whatever think of giving up.

WILLIAM LANGLAND

1330?–1400?

'On a May morning among the Malvern hills a strange
thing happened to me as if by magic . . .' So begins the
extraordinary dream of a 'field full of folk', the setting for *The
Vision of William Concerning Piers the Ploughman*—a long allegorical
poem satirizing church and society in the turbulent England of the
fourteenth century.
Its author, born in Shropshire, was a clerk in minor
orders. He scraped a meagre living for himself, his wife Kit and
daughter Nicolette, mainly by singing masses for the rich, and
occasionally by begging. From the poor side of the 'field full of folk',
he saw much at which to direct his biting humour—the excesses of
the rich, the hypocrisy of a corrupt church, the folly of popular
superstition. Although a loyal Catholic, he clearly had much
sympathy with the early reformers such as John Wycliffe.

A PROFESSIONAL PILGRIM

An illustration from the frontispiece of the first
edition of *Piers the Ploughman*.

Then a thousand men thronged together,
crying aloft to Christ and his Virgin
Mother, that Grace might go with them in
their search for Truth. But not one of them
had the wisdom to know the way. So they
blundered on like beasts, over humps and
hills, till at last, late in the day and far from
home, they met a man dressed like a
strange Saracen, as pilgrims are. He carried
a staff, with a broad strip of cloth twisted
like bindweed. By his side were slung a bag
and begging-bowl, and souvenirs were
pinned all round his hat—dozens of phials
of holy oil, scallop-shells from Galicia, and
emblems from Sinai. His cloak was sewn all
over with devices—Holy Land crosses,
cross-keys from Rome, and a St Veronica
handkerchief across the front—to let
everyone know how many shrines he had
seen.

'Where have you come from?' the
people asked.

'From Sinai', he said, 'and from Our
Lord's Sepulchre. I have also visited
Bethlehem, Babylon, Armenia, Alexandria, and many more holy places. You can
see by the signs in my hat how widely I've
travelled—on foot and in all weathers,
seeking out shrines of saints for the good of
my soul.'

'Do you know anything about a saint
called Truth?' they said. 'Can you tell us
where to find him?'

'Good Heavens, no!' said the man. 'I've
met plenty of palmers with their staffs and
scrips, but no one ever asked for a saint by
that name.'

In *Piers the Ploughman* Langland ridicules his contemporaries' delight in making
pilgrimages which were often conducted in a very light-hearted manner. This group
of pilgrims is depicted on a thirteenth-century window in Canterbury Cathedral.

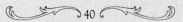

CATHERINE OF SIENA

1347–1380

The unmanageable twenty-fifth child of a prosperous
dyer, Catherine Benincasa made a vow of celibacy at eleven and at
sixteen joined a lay Dominican order. For three years she stayed in
her room, praying and speaking only to her priest. Then, feeling
called to a more active life, she began to work amongst the sick and
poor. A mixed group of young disciples gathered around her. As
her reputation for intelligence and holiness grew, she was called in
to solve political disputes, even attempting to make peace between
the pope and the secular rulers. Her letters and her book *The
Dialogue* were dictated to a scribe, for she never learned to write.

THE BRIDGE

God said: . . . No sooner had man rebelled against me than he rebelled against himself too . . . Moreover, all created things now rebelled against him, which would have obeyed him had he remained in the state in

which I had placed him . . . And no sooner had he sinned than a stormy torrent began to flow that ever buffets him with its waves, bringing him weariness and trouble from his own self, from the devil, and from the world. And you were all drowned in it because none of you, however just, could get through it to eternal life.

And so, wishing to remedy your great evils, I have given you my Son as a bridge, that you may not drown in, but pass over, the flood—the stormy sea of this dark life. See then how indebted my creature is to me, and how foolhardy it is to persist in drowning rather than accept my remedy . . . Consider the bridge that is my Son, and see how its great span reaches from heaven to earth; see, that is, how it links the grandeur of the Godhead with the clay of your humanity . . . No heaping up of earth alone could ever have sufficed to make a bridge great enough to span the torrent and open the way to eternal life . . . So my sublimity stooped to the earth of your humanity and together they made a bridge and remade the road. And why? So that you might indeed come to the joy of the angels. But it would be no use my Son's having become your bridge to life if you do not use it.

FROM 'THE DIALOGUE OF DIVINE PROVIDENCE'

For six years Catherine lived in Siena.
Here she gathered round her a circle of friends to whom she
wrote letters on many subjects.

THOMAS À KEMPIS

1380–1471

In 1374 a loose-living young Dutchman called Geert Groote experienced a sudden and dramatic conversion to Christ. Immediately he set up a small community whose members were dedicated to serving God together without taking monastic vows. They became the 'Brethren of the Common Life'. The movement founded houses all over Holland, Germany and Switzerland, well known for their piety and their contribution to education. A few years after Groote's conversion, Thomas Hemerken was born to humble parents in Kempen, near Cologne. At thirteen he was sent with his brother to the Brethren's famous school at Deventer. The brothers made a deep impression on him. 'Never before,' he wrote later, 'had I seen men so devout, so full of love for God and their fellow-men. Living in the world, they were altogether unworldly.' Under their influence, Thomas became an Augustinian canon at Zwolle, where his brother was already prior. He copied manuscripts, preached and counselled others, but most of all he wrote books. One of his writings, *The Imitation of Christ*, is a handbook teaching that the way to live the Christian life fully is to follow Christ's example. It has become the best-loved Christian book ever written and its continuing popularity is second only to that of the Bible.

FRIENDSHIP WITH JESUS

When Jesus is with us, all is well, and nothing seems hard; but when Jesus is absent, everything is difficult. When Jesus does not speak to the heart, all other comfort is unavailing; but if Jesus speaks but a single word, we are greatly comforted . . . What can the world offer you, without Jesus? To be without Jesus is hell most grievous; to be with Jesus is to know the sweetness of heaven. If Jesus is with you, no enemy can harm you. Whoever finds Jesus, finds a rich treasure, and a good above every good. He who loses Jesus, loses much indeed, and more than the whole world.

Poorest of all men is he who lives without Jesus, and richest of all is he who stands in favour with Jesus.

It is a great art to know how to hold converse with Jesus, and to know how to keep Jesus is wisdom indeed. Be humble and a man of peace, and Jesus will abide with you. But if you turn aside to worldly things, you will soon cause Jesus to leave you, and you will lose his grace. And if you drive him away and lose him, with whom may you take refuge, and whom will you seek for your friend? Without a friend, you cannot live happily, and if Jesus is not your

—LIVING IN THE PRESENT—

There was once a man who was very anxious, and wavered between fear and hope. One day, overcome with sadness, he lay prostrate in prayer before the altar in church, and pondering these matters in his mind, said, 'Oh, if only I knew that I should always persevere!' Then he heard in his heart an answer from God: 'If you knew this, what would you do? Do now what you would then, and all will be well.' So, comforted and strengthened, he committed himself to the will of God, and his anxious uncertainty vanished. Nor did he wish any longer to inquire into what would happen to him, but strove the more earnestly to learn the perfect and acceptable will of God, whenever he began or undertook any good work.

THE WAY OF THE CROSS

There is no other way to life and to true inner peace, than the way of the Cross, and of daily self-denial. Go where you will, seek what you will; you will find no higher way above nor safer way below than the road of the Holy Cross. Arrange and order all things to your own ideas and wishes, yet you will still find suffering to endure, whether you will or not; so you will always find the Cross . . . If you bear the Cross willingly, it will bear you and lead you to your desired goal, where pain shall be no more; but it will not be in this life. If you bear the cross unwillingly, you make it a burden, and load yourself more heavily; but you must needs bear it. If you cast away one cross, you will certainly find another, and perhaps a heavier . . . So long as suffering is grievous to you and you seek to escape it, so long will it go ill with you, for the trouble you try to escape will pursue you everywhere . . . Be assured of this, that you must live a dying life. And the more completely a man dies to self, the more he begins to live to God.

best friend, you will be exceedingly sad and lonely; so it is foolish to trust or delight in any other. It is better to have the whole world as your enemy, than offend Jesus. Therefore, of all dear friends, let Jesus be loved first and above all. Love all men for Jesus' sake, but Jesus for himself.

THANKFULNESS IN EVERYTHING

Be thankful for the smallest blessing, and you will deserve to receive greater. Value the least gifts no less than the greatest, and simple graces as especial favours. If you remember the dignity of the Giver, no gift will seem small or mean, for nothing can be valueless that is given by the most high God. Even if he awards punishment and pain, accept them gladly, for whatever he allows to befall us is always for our salvation.

DESIDERIUS ERASMUS

1467?–1536

Born at Rotterdam, the illegitimate son of a doctor's daughter and a priest, Erasmus was educated by the Brethren of the Common Life at Deventer. He tried the monastic life as an Augustinian canon at Steyn, and the academic life at the University of Paris, but neither was to his taste. So he took to a rather restless life of study, writing and travel. Although his satires on the corruption of the church became best sellers, he was always poor because of the amount he spent on valuable manuscripts, fine clothes and good food.

Erasmus' contributions to the revival of learning, for example, his edition of the Greek New Testament (the first to be printed), were invaluable. In works such as *The Praise of Folly*, written during a week's illness at the house of his friend Thomas More, he mixed humour with strong criticism of the status quo—in his own words, 'medicine disguised as pleasure'. Although he refused to support Luther's actions, he undoubtedly helped to hasten the Reformation—as contemporary critics put it, he 'laid the egg which Luther hatched'.

Erasmus spent many years in Basle. Here he published his edition of the Greek New Testament. The City Hall was built at the beginning of the sixteenth century, just before Erasmus moved to the city.

The sun itself is not as common and accessible to all as is Christ's teaching. It keeps no one at a distance, unless a person, begrudging himself, keeps himself away. Indeed I disagree very much with those who are unwilling that Holy Scripture, translated into the vulgar tongue, be read by the uneducated, as if Christ taught such intricate doctrines that they could scarcely be understood by very few theologians; or as if the strength of the Christian religion consisted in men's ignorance of it. The mysteries of kings, perhaps, are better concealed, but Christ wishes his mysteries published as openly as possible . . . And I would that they were translated into all languages so that they could be read and understood not only by Scots and Irish but also by Turks and Saracens. Surely the first step is to understand in one way or another. It may be that many will ridicule, but some may be taken captive. Would that, as a result, the farmer sing some portion of them at the plough, the weaver hum some parts of them to the movement of his shuttle, the traveller lighten the weariness of the journey with stories of this kind!

FROM HIS PREFACE TO THE GREEK NEW TESTAMENT

THOMAS MORE
1478–1535

According to his friend and fellow-scholar Erasmus, More had 'such a passion for jokes, that one might almost suppose he had been born for them.' One of his longer jokes was *Utopia* (or 'No-place'), the account of an imaginary island which he wrote to ridicule the follies of his own society.

More's own life provided less material for laughter. A dedicated student of history and classical literature and a devoted family man who took great care in the education of his daughters, he was reluctantly appointed to high political office because of his success as a speaker. Soon he was in head-on conflict with King Henry VIII over the king's divorce and rejection of the pope's authority. The disagreement led to More's imprisonment and eventually his execution. He met his death with his customary courage and good humour. 'I am the king's good servant,' he declared, 'but God's first.'

THE UTOPIAN'S ATTITUDE TO WEALTH

According to this system, plates and drinking-vessels, though beautifully designed, are made of quite cheap stuff like glass or earthenware. But silver and gold are the normal materials for the humblest items of domestic equipment, such as chamber-pots. They also use chains and fetters of solid gold to immobilize slaves, and anyone who commits a really shameful crime is forced to go about with gold rings on his ears and fingers, a gold necklace round his neck, and a crown of gold on his

Now I finally return to St Paul . . . From a writer of this stature you hear so many great commendations of folly. What he actually does is openly to teach that folly is necessary for the good of the town: 'Let him that seems to be wise among you become a fool, that he may be wise . . .' I do not find it out of the ordinary that Paul ascribes a certain foolishness to God himself. 'The foolishness of God', he says, 'is wiser than men' . . .

The whole of the Christian religion seems to have a certain relationship with some kind of folly but fails to agree at all with wisdom . . . What fool could possibly act more foolishly than those whom the ardour of religion has totally consumed? They throw away their wealth, they neglect injuries, permit themselves to be deceived, fail to discriminate between friend and foe, shrink from pleasure, and cram themselves with hunger, vigils, tears, labours, contumelies. They prefer death to life and, in short, seem to have grown impervious to sensation and live as if their souls no longer dwelt in their bodies. What is this other than insanity? It gives credence to the fact that the apostles seemed drunk on new wine and Paul seemed mad in the eyes of the judge Festus.

FROM 'THE PRAISE OF FOLLY'

head. In fact they do everything they can to bring these metals into contempt . . .

It's much the same with jewels. There are pearls to be found on the beaches, diamonds and garnets on certain types of rock—but they never bother to look for them. However, if they happen to come across one, they pick it up and polish it for some toddler to wear . . .

This curious convention is liable to cause some equally curious reactions, as I realized most vividly in the case of the Flatulentine diplomats. These diplomats visited Aircastle while I was there. . . When the legation arrived, it consisted of only three men, but these were escorted by a hundred retainers, all wearing multi-coloured clothes, mostly made of silk. As for the great men themselves . . . they wore cloth of gold, with great gold chains round their necks, gold ear-rings dangling from their ears, and gold rings on their fingers. Their very hats were festooned with glittering ropes of pearl and other jewels. In fact they were fully equipped with all the things used in Utopia for punishing slaves, humiliating criminals, or amusing small children.

Well, I wouldn't have missed it for anything . . . You see, from the Utopians' point of view . . . all that splendour was merely degrading. So they reserved their most respectful greeting for the least distinguished members of the party, and completely ignored the diplomats themselves, assuming from the gold chains that they were slaves.

Oh, but you should have seen the faces of the older children, who'd grown out of things like pearls and jewels, when they saw the ones on the envoys' hats. They kept nudging their mothers and whispering:

'I say, Mother, just look at that great baby! Fancy wearing jewellery at his age!'

To which the mother would reply, very seriously:

'Sh, dear! I imagine he must be a clown attached to the embassy.'

This illustration for *Utopia* (left) was taken from an engraving by Holbein.

After Martin Luther refused to recant at the Diet of Worms he
was imprisoned, for his own safety, in the Wartburg Castle. In
this room in the castle he translated the New Testament from
Greek into German.

MARTIN LUTHER

1483–1546

'Who would ever have predicted . . . that I would one day cause such heartache to my father, get into such a scrape with the pope, and marry an ex-nun?'
Many paved the way, but it was Martin Luther, a Saxon miner's son, who set the Protestant cause fully in motion. Fear of God's judgement ruled Martin's early life. This fear led him to become an Augustinian monk, after narrowly escaping death in a thunderstorm; and it still obsessed him when he became a professor of biblical studies at the University of Wittenberg.
His discovery of God's grace transformed his spiritual life. But it also brought conflict with the church of his day. When Johann Tetzel was sent to Germany by the pope to sell 'indulgences', or pardons for sins, Luther nailed ninety-five arguments on the university bulletin board. Only through faith in Christ, he declared, could forgiveness be found. The ninety-five theses, and his other writings, led to his trial before the Diet, or parliament, at Worms, which banished him from church and state. Imprisoned for his own protection, he continued to write, translating the Bible into German to make it available to the common people.
Luther's popular following was immense. People began to question everything in the church—its organization, its styles of worship, the celibacy of clergy. The Catholic church could neither stop nor contain the tide of reform.

The seal of Martin Luther.

BREAKTHROUGH TO FAITH

I had certainly been seized with a wondrous eagerness to understand Paul in the epistle to the Romans, but hitherto I had been held up . . . by one word only, in chapter 1: 'The righteousness of God is revealed.' For I hated this word 'righteousness of God', which . . . I had been taught to understand philosophically as what they call the formal or active righteousness, whereby God is just and punishes unjust sinners.

For my case was this: however irreproachable my life as a monk, I felt myself in the presence of God to be a sinner with a most unquiet conscience, nor could I believe him to be appeased by the satisfaction I could offer. I did not love—nay, I hated this just God who punishes sinners . . . And so I raged with a savage and confounded conscience; yet I knocked importunately at Paul in this place, with a parched and burning desire to know what he could mean.

At last, as I meditated day and night, God showed mercy and I turned my attention to the connection of the words, namely, 'The righteousness of God is revealed, as it is written: the righteous shall live by faith'—and there I began to understand that the righteousness of God is the righteousness in which a just man lives by the gift of God . . . in other words that by which the merciful God justifies us through faith . . . At this I felt myself straightway born afresh and to have entered through the open gates into paradise itself.

FROM THE 'AUTOBIOGRAPHICAL FRAGMENT'

THE BLESSINGS OF ANXIETY

To the saintly, anxious lady, Katherine Luther, my gracious dear wife. Grace and peace in Christ! Most saintly lady doctoress, we thank you kindly for your great care for us, which prevented you sleeping, for since you began to be so anxious we were nearly consumed by a fire in our inn just outside my room door; and yesterday, doubtless on account of your anxiety, a stone fell upon our heads and almost crushed us as in a mousetrap; and over and above, in our own private room, lime and mortar came down for two days, and when the masons came—after only touching the stone with two fingers—it fell, and was as large as a large pillow, and two hand-breadths wide. We had to thank your anxious care for all this, but happily the dear, holy angels guarded us also. I fear if you do not cease being anxious the earth may at last swallow us up and the elements pursue us. Is this how you have learned the Catechism and the faith? Pray and leave it to God to care for us, as he has promised in the fifty-fifth Psalm and many other places, 'Cast thy burden on the Lord, and he shall sustain thee.'

FROM A LETTER TO KATHERINE LUTHER

PENANCES VERSUS REPENTANCE

When our Lord and Master Jesus Christ said, 'Repent', he meant the whole life of believers to be one of repentance.

This saying cannot be taken to mean the sacrament of penance which is administered by the priesthood.

Every Christian who is truly repentant is fully cleared of penalty and guilt, even without a letter of pardon.

Christians are to be taught that a man who sees a brother in need and passes him by to give his money for the purchase of pardon wins for himself not the indulgence of the pope but the indignation of God.

FROM THE '95 THESES'

HERE I STAND

Most serene emperor, most illustrious princes: two questions were put to me yesterday by your Highness, whether I acknowledged as mine a list of books published under my name, and whether I wished to hold to my defence of them or to revoke them. I gave a deliberate and plain answer to the first, and I stand by it and always shall—namely, that the books were mine . . . However, because I am a man and not God, I can bring no other protection to my writings than my Lord Jesus Christ brought to his own teaching, when at the interrogation before Annas he was struck by a servant and said: 'If I have spoken evil, testify to the evil.' . . . Unless I am convicted by the testimony of scripture or plain reason . . . I am bound by the scriptures I have quoted, and my conscience is captive to the Word of God. I neither can nor will revoke anything, for it is neither safe nor honest to act against one's conscience. Amen.

FROM HIS REPLY TO THE DIET OF WORMS

John Calvin

1509-1564

While studying at the University of Paris, Calvin read
the newly-published writings of Martin Luther, and, in his own
words, 'God subdued and brought my heart to docility.' France was
in religious and political ferment, so Calvin fled to Basle. There, in
1536, he wrote the first version of his *Institutes of the Christian
Religion*, a mere six chapters of doctrinal instruction based on the
Ten Commandments, the Apostles' Creed and the Lord's Prayer.
The final version, finished in 1559 during an attack of malaria,
contained eighty chapters! 'I count myself one of those who write as
they learn and learn as they write', said its author.
Calvin's abilities led the city of Geneva to invite him to
promote reform there. Under the motto, 'To God alone be the
glory', he set about transforming Geneva into a model Christian
city. Church attendance was compulsory; theatre-going, shooting,
gambling, dancing, drinking and extravagant clothing were
forbidden. In spite of opposition, this strict regime did ensure peace
and prosperity for some years; and Calvin's writings provided a
clear handbook of Protestant thinking for succeeding generations.

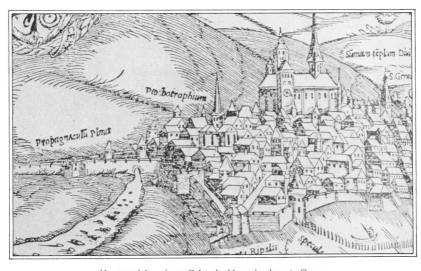

Hearing of the reforms Calvin had brought about in Geneva,
hundreds of refugees flocked to the city. When they eventually returned to their home countries they
carried with them Calvin's teaching and ideas.

ONLY THROUGH CHRIST

God, who is the highest righteousness,
cannot love the unrighteousness that he
sees in us all. All of us, therefore, have in
ourselves something deserving of God's
hatred. With regard to our corrupt nature
and the wicked life that follows it, all of us
surely displease God, are guilty in his sight,
and are born to the damnation of hell. But
because the Lord wills not to lose what is
his in us, out of his own kindness he still
finds something to love. However much
we may be sinners by our own fault, we
nevertheless remain his creatures. However much we have brought death upon

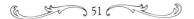

ourselves, yet he has created us unto life. Thus he is moved by pure and freely given love of us to receive us into grace. Since there is a perpetual and irreconcilable disagreement between righteousness and unrighteousness, so long as we remain sinners he cannot receive us completely. Therefore, to take away all cause for enmity and to reconcile us utterly to himself, he wipes out all evil in us by the expiation set forth in the death of Christ; that we, who were previously unclean and impure, may show ourselves righteous and holy in his sight . . . Hence, we can be fully and firmly joined with God only when Christ joins us with him. If, then, we would be assured that God is pleased with and kindly disposed towards us, we must fix our eyes and minds on Christ alone.

THE ROLE OF GOVERNMENT

To think of doing away with civil government is outrageous barbarity. Its function among men is no less than that of bread, water, sun, and air; indeed, its place of honour is far more excellent. For it does not merely see to it, as all these serve to do, that men breathe, eat, drink, and are kept

warm, even though it surely embraces all these activities when it provides for their living together. It does not, I repeat, look to this only, but also prevents idolatry, sacrilege against God's name, blasphemies against his truth, and other public offences against religion from arising and spreading among the people; it prevents the public peace from being disturbed; it provides that each man may keep his property safe and sound; that men may carry on blameless intercourse among themselves; that honesty and modesty may be preserved among men. In short, it provides that a public manifestation of religion may exist among Christians, and that humanity be maintained among men . . .

But in that obedience which we have shown to be due to the authority of rulers, we are always to make this exception, indeed, to observe it as primary, that such obedience is never to lead us away from obedience to him, to whose will the desires of all kings ought to be subject, to whose decrees all their commands ought to yield, to whose majesty their sceptres ought to be submitted . . . If they command anything against him, let it go unesteemed.

JOHN OF THE CROSS

1542–1591

If Germany was the fountainhead of the Reformation,
Spain was that of the Counter-Reformation—the Catholic church's
attempt to put its house in order. While Ignatius Loyola's Jesuits
reached outwards through education and missionary work, others
concentrated on the inward life through a revival of the mystical
way. Juan de Yepes, a Carmelite monk better known as John of the
Cross, led this movement.

Monasteries in John's day had become comfortable, even
luxurious. Inspired by his friend Teresa of Avila, John helped found
the Discalced (or 'barefoot') Carmelites, whose way of life was much
more disciplined. The official Carmelite authorities promptly
imprisoned him in a tiny cell built into the wall of Toledo prison.
Here he wrote the *Spiritual Canticle*, a long devotional poem based
on the Song of Songs.

After his escape, John eventually rose to high office in the
Carmelite administration. He wrote further mystical works in the
form of poems with detailed commentaries—*The Ascent of Mount
Carmel* and *The Dark Night of the Soul*. His special contribution
was to describe the 'dark night' of detachment from all earthly
pleasures through which the soul must pass on its way to full
union with God. John ended his days in solitary prayer, retreating
from the disputes which still plagued the Carmelite order.

FROM MILK TO SOLID FOOD

It must be known that the soul, after it has
been definitely converted to the service of
God, is, as a rule, spiritually nurtured and
caressed by God, even as is the tender child
by its loving mother, who warms it with
the heat of her bosom and nurtures it with
sweet milk and soft and pleasant food, and
carries it and caresses it in her arms; but,
as the child grows bigger, the mother
gradually ceases caressing it, and, hiding
her tender love, puts bitter aloes upon her
sweet breast, sets down the child from her
arms and makes it walk upon its feet, so
that it may lose the habits of a child . . .
The loving mother is like the grace of God,
for, as soon as the soul is regenerated by its
new warmth and fervour for the service of
God, he treats it in the same way; he makes
it to find spiritual milk, sweet and

delectable, in all the things of God,
without any labour of its own, and also
great pleasure in spiritual exercises . . . In
which things spiritual persons (though
taking part in them with great efficacy and
persistence and using and treating them
with great care) often find themselves,
spiritually speaking, very weak and imperfect. For since they are moved to these
things and to these spiritual exercises by
the consolation and pleasure that they find
in them, and since, too, they have not been
prepared for them by the practice of
earnest striving in the virtues, they have
many faults and imperfections with respect
to these spiritual actions of theirs; for after
all, any man's actions correspond to the
habit of perfection attained by him . . .

Since, then, the conduct of these

beginners upon the way of God is ignoble, and has much to do with their love of self and their own inclinations . . . God desires to lead them farther. He seeks to bring them out of that ignoble kind of love to a higher degree of love for him . . .

When they are going about these spiritual exercises with the greatest delight and pleasure, and when they believe that the sun of divine favour is shining most brightly upon them, God turns all this light of theirs into darkness, and shuts against them the door and the source of the sweet spiritual water which they were tasting in God whensoever and for as long as they desired . . . And thus he leaves them so completely in the dark that they know not whither to go . . . For, as I have said, God now sees that they have grown a little, and are becoming strong enough to lay aside their swaddling clothes and be taken from the gentle breast; so he sets them down from his arms and teaches them to walk on their own feet; which they feel to be very strange, for everything seems to be going wrong with them.

FROM 'THE DARK NIGHT OF THE SOUL'

The town of Toledo in central Spain where John of the Cross was imprisoned.

GEORGE HERBERT
1593–1633

'A book so full of plain, prudent and useful rules, that
the country parson that can spare twelve pence and yet wants it, is
scarce excusable.' Thus Izaak Walton, Herbert's biographer,
described *A Priest to the Temple, or The Country Parson, His Character
and Rule of Holy Life*, written by Herbert so that he himself might
have 'a mark to aim at' and published only after his death.
Herbert was public orator at Cambridge, and served at
the English court, before becoming a country parson at Bemerton
in Wiltshire. His poems, some of the most sincere and well-loved
Christian poetry ever written, were best sellers even in his lifetime.
But to the people of Bemerton he was simply a caring,
unpretentious 'shepherd of the flock', who made every effort to live
up to the portrait of the ideal parson he had painted.

THE PARSON VISITING

The country parson upon the afternoons in the weekdays, takes occasion sometimes to visit in person, now one quarter of his parish, now another. For there he shall find his flock most naturally as they are, wallowing in the midst of their affairs; whereas on Sunday it is easy for them to compose themselves to order . . . When he comes to any house, first he blesses it, and then as he finds the persons of the house employed, so he forms his discourse. Those that he finds religiously employed, he both commends them much, and furthers them when he is gone, in their employment; if he

finds them reading, he furnishes them with good books; if curing poor people, he supplies them with recipes, and instructs them further in that skill, showing them how acceptable such works are to God.

Those that he finds busy in the works of their calling, he commends also; for it is a good and just thing for everyone to do their own business. But then he admonishes them of two things; first that they dive not too deep into worldly affairs . . . but that they so labour, as neither to labour anxiously, nor distrustfully, nor profanely. They labour anxiously, when they overdo it, to the loss of their quiet and health; distrustfully, when they doubt God's providence, thinking that their own labour is the cause of their thriving . . . profanely, when they set themselves to work like brute beasts, never raising their thoughts to God, nor sanctifying their labour with daily prayer . . .

Secondly, he advises them so to labour for wealth . . . as they make not that the end of their labour, but that they may have wherewithal to serve God the better, and to do good deeds.

THE PARSON PREACHING

The country parson preaches constantly, the pulpit is his joy and his throne . . . When he preaches, he procures attention by all possible art, both by earnestness of speech, it being natural to men to think, that where is much earnestness, there is something worth hearing; and by a diligent cast of his eye upon his auditors . . . and with particularizing of his speech now to the younger sort, then to the elder, now to the poor, and now to the rich. This is for you, and this is for you; for particulars ever touch, and awake more than generalities . . .

Sometimes he tells them stories, and sayings of others, according as his text invites them; for them also men heed, and remember better than exhortations; which though earnest, yet often die with the sermon, especially with country people; which are thick, and heavy, and hard to raise to a point of zeal . . . and need a mountain of fire to kindle them; but stories and sayings they will well remember . . .

BROTHER LAWRENCE

1611?–1691

Born in Lorraine, Nicholas Herman joined the army in
his teens but was invalided out with a leg wound. He became
footman to the treasurer of the exchequer, but was, in his own
words, 'a big heavy-handed fellow who broke everything'! Wishing
to atone for his clumsiness and mistakes, in middle age he entered a
Discalced Carmelite monastery, taking the name Brother Lawrence.
After four years of severe doubts he lived in unbroken contentment
—a fact with which he often reproached God, as he had wanted to
suffer for him! He worked for fifteen years in the kitchens and then
in the cobbler's workshop; but everywhere was a place of
prayer to him.

In 1666 Lawrence's reputation for godliness came to the
ears of his archbishop. He sent his vicar-general, the Abbé de
Beaufort, to investigate this obscure monk. The Abbé wrote notes
of their conversations, collected Lawrence's letters and wrote a
memoir after his death. Together, these papers formed *The Practice
of the Presence of God*, which has inspired countless Christians to
start a closer walk with God.

___CONVERSATIONS WITH___ A HOLY MAN

The day I first saw Brother Lawrence he
told me that God had granted him extraordinary grace in his conversion at the age
of eighteen years . . . One day in winter,
while looking at a tree stripped of its leaves,
and reflecting that after a time its leaves
would appear again and then flowers and
fruits, he received a lofty view of the
providence and the power of God which
has never been effaced from his soul. This
view drew him altogether from the world,
and gave him such a love for God that he
was unable to say whether it had increased
during the span of forty years since he had
received this grace . . .

We should, he said, fix ourselves firmly
in the presence of God by conversing all
the time with him. A shameful course it
would be to abandon his fellowship to give
thought to trifles. We should feed our soul
with a lofty conception of God and from
that derive great joy in being his . . .

When he set himself the task of putting
some virtue into practice, he would address

himself to God, saying: 'God, I should not be able to do that unless you enabled me to do it', and then he was given immediately the strength to do it and more besides. When he had fallen short, he said, he would do nothing else but confess his shortcoming and say to God, 'I should never do anything else if you left me to do it. It is yours to prevent me from falling and to set right that which is not well.' After that he concerned himself no more over his fault . . .

He had been sent off a few days earlier to Burgundy for stocks of wine, a painful task for him as he had no aptitude for business, was lame in one leg, and could only get about the boat by rolling himself over the casks. He did not, however, trouble himself about this, no more than about his whole purchase of wine. He told God that it was his business, after which he found that everything worked out and worked out well . . .

The time of prayer was, he said, in no way different for him than any other. He would observe his times of withdrawal when the Father Prior bade him do so, but he neither wanted nor asked for them, because his most demanding work did not divert him from God.

RICHARD BAXTER

1615–1691

The seventeenth century was one of the most unsettled times of English history, with a civil war followed by a short-lived republic. Richard Baxter was deeply involved in the nation's troubles. Yet in the midst of it he wrote *The Saints' Everlasting Rest*, a long treatise on the joys promised to faithful Christians, for which he has been called 'the creator of popular Christian literature'.

Despite his lack of university education, Baxter became an Anglican priest and served as precentor, or director of music, at Kidderminster. His political and religious views led him to support Cromwell in the Civil War and to act as his adviser during the Commonwealth. Yet on the restoration of the monarchy in 1660 he became chaplain to Charles II. Two years later, however, the Act of Uniformity demanded that all clergy swear allegiance to the current practices of the Church of England. Baxter's views prevented him from doing this, and so he was forbidden to preach.

In 1685, elderly and ill, he was imprisoned by the notorious Judge Jeffreys for eighteen months. Not until 1689, under the Act of Toleration, was he allowed to preach again; and two years later he died.

A scene from the battle of Naseby, one of the decisive battles in the English Civil War.

CHRISTIAN MEDITATION

I call it the acting of *all* the powers of the soul to distinguish it from the common meditation of students, which is usually the mere employment of the brain. It is not a bare thinking that I mean, nor the mere use of imagination or memory, but a business of a higher and more excellent nature. When truth is apprehended only as truth, this is but a savourless and loose apprehension; but when it is apprehended as good, as well as true, this is a firm and delightful apprehension. As man is not so prone to live according to the truth he knows unless it deeply affects him, so neither does his soul enjoy its sweetness unless speculation passes into affection. The understanding is not the whole soul, and therefore cannot do the whole work . . .

This is it that has deceived Christians in this business; they have thought that meditation is nothing but the bare thinking on truths and the rolling of them in the understanding and memory . . . Therefore this is the great task in hand, and this is the work that I would set you on: to get these truths from your head to your heart . . . So much as your understanding and affections are sincerely acted upon by God, so much do you enjoy him; and this is the happy work of this meditation . . . If in this work of meditation you exercise knowledge, and gifts, and faith in miracles, and do not exercise love and joy, you do nothing . . . If your meditation tends to fill your note-book with notions and good sayings concerning God, and not your heart with longings after him, and delight in him, for all I know your book is as much a Christian as you are.

Blaise Pascal

1623–1662

A delicate, precocious child, Pascal suffered all his life
from violent headaches (a post-mortem found his skull had not
formed properly). Because of this his wealthy father kept him from
his books; so the young Blaise worked out Pythagoras' theorem
on his own! He was to become one of the foremost mathematicians
of his time. While still in his teens he made discoveries in geometry
and calculus; by using dice he worked out the theory of probability;
he designed the first mechanical computer (today there is a
computer language named after him). In physics he advanced the
knowledge of the vacuum and discovered 'Pascal's Law', the
principle of hydraulics. He is also said to have planned the first
public omnibus system!
Together with his sister, Blaise joined the Jansenists, a
reform movement within the French Catholic church, and wrote
his *Provincial Letters* in defence of their doctrines, which had caused
much controversy. In 1654 he went through a 'second conversion'
in which he was overwhelmed for two hours by 'certainty, joy and
peace'. After his death his account of this experience was found
stitched into the coat he always wore. Also found among his papers
were twenty-seven bundles of loose sheets arranged under general
headings. These were his notes for a major book defending the
Christian faith against the growing rationalism of his day. They
were published as *Pensées* (Thoughts) and became a classic of
Christian thinking.

THE WAGER

'Either God exists, or he does not.' But which side shall we take? Reason cannot decide for us one way or the other; we are separated by an infinite gulf. A game is on, at the other side of this infinite distance, where either heads or tails will turn up. Which will you gamble on? . . .

Let us weigh the gain and the loss in betting that God exists . . . If you win, you win everything; if you lose, you lose nothing. Do not hestitate, then: gamble on his existence . . .

You want to come to faith, but you do not know the way. You would like to cure yourself of unbelief, and you ask for remedies. Learn from those who were once bound and gagged like you, and who now stake all that they possess. These are the people who know the road you wish to follow; they are cured of the disease of which you wish to be cured. Follow the way by which they set out: by acting as though they already believed . . .

Now what harm will come to you if you follow this course? You will be faithful, honest, humble, grateful, generous, a sincere friend, truthful. Certainly you will not enjoy those poisonous pleasures, ambition and luxury. But will you not have others? I tell you that you will gain in this life, and that at every step you take along this road you will see so great an assurance of gain, and so little in what you risk, that you will finally realize you have gambled on something certain and infinite, which has cost you nothing.

THE CHRISTIAN GOD

The God of Christians is not a God who is simply the author of geometrical truths, or of the order of the elements; that is the view of pagans and Epicureans. He is not merely a God who exercises his providence over the lives and fortunes of men, to bestow on those who worship him a long and happy life.

The God of Abraham, the God of Isaac, the God of Jacob, the God of Christians is a God of love and comfort, a God who fills the soul and heart of those whom he possesses, a God who makes them conscious of their inward wretchedness, and his infinite mercy; who unites himself to their inmost soul, who fills it with humility and joy, with confidence and love, who renders them incapable of any other end than himself.

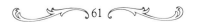

MAN AND GOD

The greatness of man is that he knows himself to be miserable. A tree does not know itself to be miserable. The miseries themselves prove man's greatness. They are the miseries of a great lord, of a deposed king . . .

The man who knows God but does not know his own misery, becomes proud. The man who knows his own misery but does not know God, ends in despair . . . The knowledge of Jesus Christ constitutes the middle course because in him we find both God and our own misery. Jesus Christ is therefore a God whom we approach without pride, and before whom we humble ourselves without despair.

FAITH IS OF THE HEART

The heart has its reasons of which reason knows nothing. We feel it in a thousand things. I say that the heart naturally loves the Universal Being, and naturally loves itself; and it gives itself to one or the other, and hardens itself against one or the other, as it chooses . . . It is the heart that feels God, not the reason; this is faith.

SEEKING AND FINDING

Jesus says: Console yourself, you would not seek me, if you had not found me.

LAW AND GRACE

The law required what it could not give. Grace gives that which it requires.

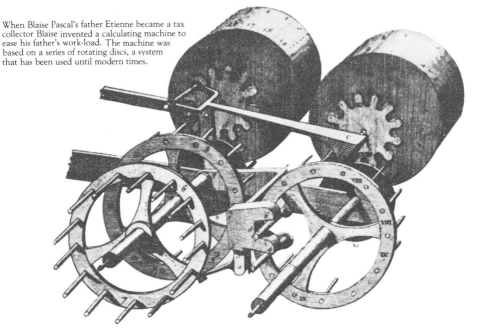

When Blaise Pascal's father Etienne became a tax collector Blaise invented a calculating machine to ease his father's work-load. The machine was based on a series of rotating discs, a system that has been used until modern times.

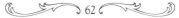

GEORGE FOX
1624–1691

'An original, being no man's copy' was the verdict on
Fox of his disciple William Penn. A weaver's son from
Leicestershire, in the heart of England, at about twenty Fox left
home in search of a deeper faith. The advice given by the clergy he
visited was less than satisfactory. 'Take tobacco and sing psalms',
suggested one. Then in a direct and powerful experience of God, he
began to realize how the 'inner light' of the Holy Spirit can
transform the Christian from within. He travelled widely,
preaching the Christ who had 'opened the door of light and life'
to him. Soon a popular movement, numbering thousands, grew
up around Fox. These people called themselves the 'Society of
Friends', but were nicknamed 'Quakers' because they sometimes
shook with emotion during worship. They met in private houses
and had no formal leadership—paid priests were regarded as
'hirelings' who treated God's truth as a saleable commodity.
Committed pacifists, they were fearless in the face of persecution.
Fox himself answered someone who brandished a sword at him by
exclaiming, 'Alack for thee, it's no more to me than a straw.' His
Journal records vividly the courage and Christlikeness of the early
Quakers. In his favourite phrase, 'The power of God was over all.'

THE LIGHT OF CHRIST

Now was I come up in spirit through the
flaming sword, into the paradise of God.
All things were new, and all the creation
gave another smell unto me than before,
beyond what words can utter. I knew
nothing but pureness, and innocency, and
righteousness, being renewed up into the
image of God by Christ Jesus, to the state
of Adam, which he was in before he fell . . .
Great things did the Lord lead me into,
and wonderful depths were opened unto
me beyond what can by words be declared
. . . He shewed me that the physicians were
out of the wisdom of God, by which the
creatures were made; and so knew not their
virtues . . . He shewed me that the priests
were out of the true faith, which Christ is
the author of; the faith which purifies and
gives victory, and brings people to have
access to God, and by which they please
God . . . He shewed me also, that the
lawyers were out of the equity, and out of
the true justice, and out of the law of God
. . . And as the Lord opened these things
unto me, I felt his power went forth over
all, by which all might be reformed, if they
would receive and bow to it. The priests
might be reformed and brought into the
true faith, which was the gift of God. The
lawyers might be reformed and brought
into the law of God, which answers that of
God which is transgressed in everyone, and
brings to love one's neighbour as himself
. . . The physicians might be reformed and

brought into the wisdom of God by which all things were made and created, that they might receive a right understanding of the creatures and understand their virtues . . .

These things I did not see by the help of man, nor by the letter, though they are written in the letter, but I saw them in the light of the Lord Jesus Christ, and by his immediate spirit and power, as did the holy men of God by whom the Holy Scriptures were written. Yet I had no slight esteem of the Holy Scriptures, but they were very precious to me, for I was in that Spirit by which they were given forth; and what the Lord opened to me I afterwards found was agreeable to them . . . With and by this divine power and Spirit of God, and the light of Jesus, I was to bring people off from all their own ways, to Christ, the new and living way; and from their own churches, which men had made and gathered, to the church in God, the general assembly written in heaven which Christ is the head of . . . And I was to bring people off from all the world's religions, which are vain; that they might know the pure religion, might visit the fatherless, the widows, and the strangers, and keep themselves from the spots of the world; that there would be not so many beggars, the sight of whom often grieved my heart, to see so much hard-heartedness amongst them that professed the name of Christ.

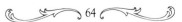

(Above) One day George Fox had a vision of 'a people to be gathered to the Lord'. After that he preached wherever people would listen.

The Quaker Meeting House at Old Jordans, Buckinghamshire, England. Quakers rejected organized churches and services, choosing instead to follow the 'inward light' of God's guidance.

John Bunyan

1628–1688

'As I walked through the wilderness of this world, I
lighted on a certain place, where was a den; and I laid me down in
that place to sleep: and as I slept I dreamed a dream.' The 'den' was
the Bedfordshire county jail where Bunyan was imprisoned for
unlicensed preaching and the 'dream' was *The Pilgrim's Progress*, the classic
story of Christian's journey from the City of Destruction to the Celestial City.
Born in the small English village of Elstow, Bunyan
followed his father's trade as a tinker. After serving in Cromwell's
army during the Civil War, he married. The couple were 'as poor as
poor might be, with not so much household stuff as a dish or spoon
betwixt us'; but his wife brought with her two religious books,
which started Bunyan's search for God. There followed a long
period of doubt and torment, related in his autobiography *Grace
Abounding to the Chief of Sinners*, and personified as Giant Despair
of Doubting Castle in *The Pilgrim's Progress*.
When at last he found peace with God, Bunyan became
a travelling preacher. But once Cromwell's Puritan-led Republic
ended in 1660, Bunyan's refusal to conform to the Anglican
church's requirements meant twelve years in prison. There he wrote
his main works, *The Pilgrim's Progress*, the story of Christian's journey, becoming
an immediate best seller. Bunyan died of a chill caught going out to reconcile a
father and son—just before the Act of Toleration brought the
religious freedom for which he had longed.

CHRISTIAN LOSES HIS BURDEN

Now I saw in my dream, that the highway up which Christian was to go, was fenced on either side with a Wall, and that Wall is called Salvation. Up this way therefore did burdened Christian run, but not without great difficulty, because of the load on his back.

He ran thus till he came at a place somewhat ascending; and upon that place stood a Cross, and a little below in the bottom, a sepulchre. So I saw in my dream, that just as Christian came up with the Cross, his burden loosed from off his shoulders, and fell from off his back; and began to tumble, and so continued to do till it came to the mouth of the sepulchre, where it fell in, and I saw it no more.

Then was Christian glad and lightsome, and said with a merry heart, 'He hath given me rest, by his sorrow, and life, by his death.' Then he stood still a while, to look and wonder; for it was very surprising to him that the sight of the Cross should thus ease him of his burden. He looked therefore, and looked again, even till the springs that were in his head sent the waters down his cheeks. Now as he stood looking and weeping, behold three Shining Ones came to him, and saluted him, with 'Peace be to thee.' So the first said to him, 'Thy sins be forgiven.' The second stripped him of his rags, and clothed him with change of raiment. The third also set a mark on his forehead, and gave him a roll with a seal upon it, which he bid him look on as he ran, and that he should give it in at the Celestial Gate; so they went their way. Then Christian gave three leaps for joy, and went on singing . . .

During his imprisonment in Bedford jail John Bunyan wrote a number of books including *The Pilgrim's Progress*.

FAITHFUL'S TEMPTATION

Faithful When I came to the foot of the Hill called Difficulty, I met with a very aged man, who asked me what I was, and whither bound? I told him that I was a pilgrim, going to the Celestial City. Then said the old man, 'Thou lookest like an honest fellow; wilt thou be content to dwell with me, for the wages that I shall give thee?' Then I asked him his name, and where he dwelt. He said his name was 'Adam the First, and I dwell in the town of Deceit.' I asked him then, What was his work? And what the wages that he would give? He told me, that his work was many delights and his wages, that I should be his heir at last. I further asked him what house he kept, and what other servants he had. So he told me that his house was maintained with all the dainties in the world, and that his servants were those of his own begetting. Then I asked how many children he had; he said, that he had but three daughters, The Lust of the Flesh, The Lust of the Eyes, and The Pride of Life, and that I should marry them all if I would. Then I asked how long he would have me live with him. And he told me, as long as he lived himself.

Christian Well, and what conclusion came the old man and you to at last?

Faithful Why, at first I found myself somewhat inclinable to go with the man,

An eighteenth-century engraving of John Bunyan dreaming *The Pilgrim's Progress*, with Christian fleeing the City of Destruction.

The Pilgrim's Progress vividly describes the Christian's journey
through life. In this illustration Christian sets off with his load of ˙sin on his back.

for I thought he spake very fair; but looking in his forehead as I talked with him I saw there written, 'Put off the old man with his deeds.'

Christian And how then?

Faithful Then it came burning hot into my mind, whatever he said and however he flattered when he got me home to his house he would sell me for a slave. So I bid him forbear to talk, for I would not come near the door of his house . . . So I went on my way up the Hill.

Now, when I had got about half way up, I looked behind me, and saw one coming after me, swift as the wind . . . As soon as the man overtook me, he was but a word and a blow; for down he knocked me and laid me for dead. But when I was a little come to myself again, I asked him wherefore he served me so. He said, 'Because of my secret inclining to Adam the First', and with that he struck me another deadly blow on the breast, and beat me down backward; so I lay at his foot as dead as before. So when I came to myself again, I cried him mercy; but he said, 'I know not how to show mercy', and with that knocked me down again. He had doubtless made an end of me, but that one came by and bid him forbear.

Christian Who was that, that bid him forbear?

Faithful I did not know him at first, but as he went by, I perceived the holes in his hands, and his side; then I concluded that he was our Lord. So I went up the Hill.

Christian That man that overtook you was Moses, he spareth none, neither knoweth he how to show mercy to those that transgress his law.

Faithful I know it very well, it was not the first time that he has met with me. 'Twas he that came to me when I dwelt securely at home, and that told me he would burn my house over my head, if I stayed there.

The village green at Elstow, in Bedfordshire, where John Bunyan was born. Before his conversion, when he was convicted of sin, he was troubled that he had played the ball-game 'cat' here on Sundays, and so broken the Sabbath.

MADAME GUYON
1648–1717

An introspective and deeply religious girl, Jeanne Marie
Bouvier de la Mothe wanted to be a nun. But when she was sixteen
her mother pressurized her into marrying Jacques Guyon, an
invalid twenty-two years her senior.
After seven years of marriage Guyon died, and Jeanne
came under the influence of Père Lacombe, an unstable and
eccentric priest. She spent several years travelling around France
with him, preaching and teaching, until both were arrested on
suspicion of heresy and immorality. Madame Guyon was released
by the intervention of Madame de Maintenon, and became very
popular in royal circles. But her teaching continued to cause violent
disputes, notably between the theologians Fénelon and Bossuet.
Her demand for an inquiry to clear her name led instead to
another imprisonment, which lasted until she agreed to submit to
the church authorities.
In spite of all this controversy, her books, especially
A Short and Easy Method of Prayer, have enjoyed lasting popularity.
They made contemplative prayer accessible to many who would
never read more academic works on the subject.

—PRAYING LIKE A CHILD—

There are two kinds of people that keep silence; the one because they have nothing to say, the other because they have too much: it is so with the soul in this state: the silence is occasioned by the superabundance of matter, too great for utterance . . . The infant hanging at the mother's breast is a lively illustration of our subject: it begins to draw the milk by moving its little lips; but when the milk flows abundantly, it is content to swallow, and suspends its suction; by doing otherwise it would only hurt itself, spill the milk, and be obliged to quit the breast.

We must act in like manner in the beginning of prayer, by exerting the lips of the affections; but as soon as the milk of divine grace flows freely, we have nothing to do but, in repose and stillness, sweetly to imbibe it; and when it ceases to flow, we must again stir up the affections as the infant moves its lips . . .

But what becomes of this child, who gently and without motion drinks in the milk? . . . It drops gently asleep on its mother's bosom. So the soul that is tranquil and peaceful in prayer, sinks frequently into a mystic slumber, wherein all its powers are at rest . . .

The interior is not a stronghold to be taken by storm and violence but a kingdom of peace, which is to be gained only by love.

——MEDITATIVE READING——

Whatever truth you have chosen, read only a small portion of it, endeavouring to taste and digest it, to extract the essence and substance thereof, and proceed no farther while any savour or relish remains in the passage: when this subsides, take up your book again and proceed as before, seldom reading more than half a page at a time; for it is not the quantity that is read, but the manner of reading, that yields us profit.

Those who read fast reap no more advantage than a bee would by only skimming over the surface of the flower, instead of waiting to penetrate into it, and extract its sweets.

——WHEN WE HAVE FALLEN——

On the commission of a fault it is of great importance to guard against vexation and disquietude, which springs from a secret root of pride and a love of our own excellence; we are hurt by feeling what we are; and if we discourage ourselves or despond, we are the more enfeebled; and from our reflections on the fault a chagrin arises, which is often worse than the fault itself.

The truly humble soul is not surprised at defects or failings; and the more miserable and wretched it beholds itself, the more doth it abandon itself unto God, and press for a nearer and more intimate acquaintance with him, that it may avail itself of his eternal strength.

COTTON MATHER

1663–1728

Mather belonged to an eminent Boston Puritan family;
his father was Increase Mather, President of Harvard College and
the foremost New England cleric of his day. When Cotton entered
Harvard at twelve, he could already read Greek, Latin and Hebrew
and had mastered most of the Greek New Testament. But because
of a bad stammer he felt unsuited for the ministry and instead
studied medicine. However, by 1680 he had overcome the stammer
and begun a preaching career.
Intense, ambitious and sometimes tyrannical, Mather
played a leading part in the notorious Salem witch trials of 1692.
But he also had a keen interest in scientific investigation and was
one of the first few Americans to be elected to the Royal Society
in London. He was a passionate advocate of smallpox inoculation,
to the extent that an angry opponent once retaliated by throwing
a bomb through his window! He wrote over 400 books, of which
the best known is *Magnalia Christi Americana*, a carefully-
documented history of God's work in New England.

THE WONDERS OF CREATION

The contrivance of our most glorious Creator, in the vegetables growing upon this globe, cannot be wisely observed without admiration and astonishment. We will single out some remarkables, and glorify our God! . . .

Every particular part of the plant has its astonishing uses. The roots give it a stability, and fetch the nourishment into it, which lies in the earth ready for it. The fibres contain and convey the sap which carries up that nourishment. The plant has also larger vessels, which entertain the proper and specific juice of it; and others to carry the air for its necessary respiration. The outer and inner bark defend it from annoyances, and contribute to its augmentation. The leaves embrace and preserve the flower and fruit as they come to their explication. But the principal use of them . . . is to concoct and prepare the sap for the nourishment of the fruit, and of the whole plant; not only that which ascends from the root, but also what they take in from without, from the dew, and from the rain . . .

How agreeable the shade of plants, let every man say that sits under his own vine, and under his own fig-tree! How charming the proportion and pulchritude of the leaves, the flowers, the fruits . . . Our Saviour says of the lilies . . . that Solomon in all his glory was not arrayed like one of these. And it is observed . . . that the art of the most skilful painter cannot so mingle and temper his colours, as exactly to imitate of counterfeit the native ones of the flowers or vegetables . . .

The anatomy of plants, as it has been exhibited by the incomparable curiosity of Dr Grew, what a vast field of wonders does it lead us into! . . . Gentlemen of leisure, consult my illustrious Doctor, peruse his *Anatomy of Plants*, ponder his numberless discoveries; but all the while consider that rare person as inviting you to join with him in adoring the God . . . who has done these excellent things, which ought to be known in all the earth.

FROM 'THE CHRISTIAN PHILOSOPHER'

A botanical drawing of hemlock. Cotton Mather saw in the complex structure of plants the wonderful work of God the Creator.

JEAN PIERRE DE CAUSSADE

1675–1751

'A man who is master of his subject, passionately in
earnest about it and passionately eager to communicate it to
others', is one critic's impression of de Caussade. At only nineteen,
in training for the Jesuit priesthood at Toulouse, he was already
teaching others classics. Later he taught grammar, physics
and logic. But his true vocation, that of a spiritual guide, did
not become fully apparent until after his death when the nuns
of Nancy, to whom he had been spiritual director, put together
the notes of the lectures he had given them. These were circulated
under the title *Self-Abandonment to Divine Providence*. The work
soon became popular, for de Caussade's insights had been forged in
the fires of experience—not least his struggle with growing blindness. It was not until 1861 that *Self-Abandonment* was edited into its
final form. Since then it has gone through no less than twenty-five
editions.

THE GOSPEL OF THE HOLY SPIRIT

The Holy Spirit . . . writes his own gospel,
and he writes it in the hearts of the faithful.
All the actions, all the moments of the
saints make up the gospel of the Holy
Spirit. Their holy souls are the paper, their
sufferings and their actions are the ink.
The Holy Spirit, with his own action for
pen, writes a living gospel, but it will not be
readable until the day of glory when it will
be taken out of the printing press of this life
and published.

What a beautiful history! What a fine
book the Holy Spirit is writing now! The
book is in the press, there is no day on
which the letters which make it up are not
being composed, on which the ink is not
applied and the sheets printed. But we
dwell in the night of faith; the paper is

blacker than the ink, the characters are all
in confusion; the language is not of this
world, nothing can be understood of it.
You will be able to read this book only in
heaven.

Teach me, Divine Spirit, to read in this
book of life! I wish to become your disciple
and like a simple child believe what I
cannot see. Enough for me that my master
speaks. He says so-and-so, he groups the
letters of the book like this, he makes
himself understood in that way; it is
enough, I judge according to what he says. I
do not see why but he is the infallible truth,
all that he says or does is truthful. He wills
that this word should be composed of so
many letters, that that word should need
another number . . . Everything is signifi-
cant, there is a perfect meaning everywhere
. . . I believe this now, and when the day of
glory reveals so many mysteries to me, I
shall see what at present I can only understand confusedly, and what now seems
to me so complicated, so haphazard and
imaginary will entrance and charm me
eternally by its beauty, by the order,
reason, wisdom and incomprehensible
wonders that I shall find in it.

WILLIAM LAW

1686–1761

'The light flowed so mightily upon my soul that everything appeared in a new view.' Such was John Wesley's reaction to reading Law's *A Serious Call to a Devout and Holy Life*, in which the author, largely through a series of satirical 'portraits', attacks the formal, hypocritical religion of his day.

Law, the son of a devout grocer from the English Midlands, studied at Cambridge, was ordained and became a Fellow of his college. But in 1715, as a supporter of the Stuart cause, he refused to swear allegiance to the Hanoverian George I as head of the church. This barred him from any church or university post. So he became private tutor to a rich merchant's son, Edward Gibbon, father of the famous historian.

In 1740 Law returned to his home town of Kingscliffe to set up a small community with two friends, one a maiden lady and the other a widow. They lived under a discipline of regular prayer, Bible study and works of charity, founding schools, almshouses and libraries out of their joint income of £3,000 a year— a large sum at that time. Through his reading of Madame Guyon and her contemporaries, the medieval German mystics and the Protestant visionary Jacob Boehme, Law became more of a mystic in his later days. *A Serious Call*, however, published in 1729, emphasizes practical religion and its effects in the everyday world.

THE BUSINESSMAN

Calidus has traded above thirty years in the greatest city of the kingdom. Every hour of the day is with him an hour of business, and though he eats and drinks very heartily, yet every meal seems to be in a hurry, and he would say grace if he had time. Calidus ends every day at the tavern, but has not leisure to be there till near nine o'clock. He is always forced to drink a good hearty glass, to drive thoughts of business out of his head, and make his spirits drowsy enough for sleep. He does business all the time that he is rising, and has settled several matters before he can get to his counting-room. His prayers are a short ejaculation or two, which he never misses in stormy, tempestuous weather, because he has always something or other at sea. Calidus will tell you, with great pleasure, that he has been in this hurry for so many years, and that it must have killed him long ago, but that it has been a rule with him to get out of the town every Saturday, and make the Sunday a day of quiet, and good refreshment in the country.

He is now so rich, that he would leave off his business, and amuse his old age, with building, and furnishing a fine house

in the country, but that he is afraid he would grow melancholy if he was to quit his business . . . If thoughts of religion happen at any time to steal into his head, Calidus contents himself with thinking, that he never was a friend to heretics and infidels, that he has always been civil to the minister of his parish, and very often given something to the charity schools.

Now this way of life is at such a distance from all the doctrine and discipline of Christianity, that no one can live in it through ignorance or frailty. Calidus can no more imagine that he is 'born again of the Spirit'; that he lives here as a stranger and a pilgrim, setting his affection on things above, and laying up treasure in heaven—he can no more imagine this, than he can think that he has been all his life an apostle working miracles, and preaching the gospel.

William Law was educated at Emmanuel College, Cambridge. He was elected a Fellow in 1711 but four years later was deprived of this position because he would not swear allegiance to George I.

———FROM 'A SERIOUS CALL TO A DEVOUT AND HOLY LIFE'———

JONATHAN EDWARDS
1703–1758

The precocious son of a Connecticut pastor, at eleven Edwards had already written scientific papers on spiders and on the rainbow. At twelve he entered the new college at Yale, where he became a Master of Arts at twenty and a tutor at twenty-one. By this time he had dedicated his life to God and had spent some time as a Presbyterian minister in New York.

In 1727, Edwards became associate pastor of the Congregational church in Northampton, Massachusetts. Here, largely as a result of his preaching, there was a dramatic revival in 1735–37, which spread all over New England. In *A Faithful Narrative of the Surprising Work of God*, Edwards described the transforming effect this had on the life of the area.

Unfortunately, Edwards and his congregation disagreed on the criteria for full church membership, and in 1750 he was dismissed. He spent several years as a missionary, working largely among the American Indians, in a small frontier village. During this time he wrote an important treatise on the *Freedom of the Will*. In 1758 he was elected president of the College of New Jersey at Princeton, but just after taking up his appointment he died of smallpox.

The publication of *A Faithful Narrative* which told of the revival in Northampton, Massachusetts, encouraged ministers to look for a similar revival. Soon there was a reawakening of religious fervour throughout New England.

REVIVAL IN NORTHAMPTON

There was scarcely a single person in the town, old or young, left unconcerned about the great things of the eternal world. Those who were wont to be the vainest, and loosest; and those who had been most disposed to think, and speak slightly of . . . religion, were now generally subject to great awakenings. And the work of conversion was carried on in a most astonishing manner, and increased more and more; souls did as it were come by flocks to Jesus Christ. From day to day, for many months together, might be seen evident instances of sinners brought out of darkness into marvellous light, and delivered out of a horrible pit, and from the miry clay, and set upon a rock with a new song of praise to God in their mouths . . .

It was a time of joy in families on account of salvation being brought unto them; parents rejoicing over their children as new born, and husbands over their wives, and wives over their husbands . . . God's day was a delight . . . the congregation was alive in God's service, every hearer eager to drink in the words of the minister as they came from his mouth; the assembly in general were, from time to time, in tears while the word was preached; some weeping with sorrow and distress, others with joy and love, others with pity and concern for the souls of their neighbours . . . In all companies, on other days, on whatever occasions persons met together, Christ was to be heard of and seen in the midst of them.

FROM 'A FAITHFUL NARRATIVE OF THE SURPRISING WORK OF GOD'

JOHN WESLEY

1703–1791

'What happened in that little room was of more
importance to England than all the victories of Pitt by land or sea,'
commented one writer on Wesley's conversion.
The fifteenth son of a Lincolnshire clergyman, Wesley
was saved from a house fire as a child and always saw himself as 'a
brand plucked from the burning.' Influenced by their saintly
mother Susanna and by books such as *The Imitation of Christ* and
Jeremy Taylor's *Holy Living and Holy Dying*, John and his brother
Charles started a 'Holy Club' among their fellow-students at
Oxford. Later they both went as missionaries to Georgia. But John
had no peace about his relationship to God—until the
'Aldersgate experience' described below.
From then on, following the lead of his friend George
Whitefield, Wesley became an open-air preacher. His sermons, and
Charles' hymns, reached thousands of the working classes who had
rejected the respectable bourgeois church of their day. The new
believers drew much opposition from the established church, and
were even physically attacked by their opponents. Wesley describes
their struggles vividly in his *Journal*. To encourage each other, they
met in small local 'classes', which were to become the Methodist
church. When the Industrial Revolution came, this system of
mutual help, practical as well as spiritual, contributed much to the
development of trade unions and the Labour movement.

'STRANGELY WARMED'

All the time that I was at Savannah, I was
. . . beating the air. Being ignorant of the
righteousness of Christ, which, by a living
faith in him, bringeth salvation 'to everyone that believeth', I sought to establish my
own righteousness.

In this vile abject state of bondage to
sin, I was indeed fighting continually, but
not conquering. Before, I had willingly
served sin; now it was unwillingly; but still
I served it. I fell and rose, and fell again.
Sometimes I was overcome, and in heavi-
ness; sometimes I overcame, and was in joy.
For as in the former state I had some
foretastes of the terrors of the law, so had I
in this of the comforts of the gospel. During
this whole struggle between nature and
grace, which had now continued about ten
years, I had many remarkable returns to
prayer, especially when I was in trouble; I
had many sensible comforts, which are
indeed no other than short anticipations of
the life of faith. But I was still 'under the
law', not 'under grace'.

In the evening (of Wednesday May
24th), I went very unwillingly to a society
in Aldersgate Street, where one was reading Luther's preface to the Epistle to the
Romans. About a quarter before nine,
while he was describing the change which
God works in the heart through faith in
Christ, I felt my heart strangely warmed. I
felt I did trust in Christ, Christ alone, for
salvation; and an assurance was given me
that he had taken away my sins, even
mine, and saved me from the law of sin and
death.

THE NEW BIRTH

Before a child is born into the world he has eyes, but sees not; he has ears, but does not hear. He has a very imperfect use of any other sense. He has no knowledge of any of the things of the world, or any natural understanding. To that manner of existence which he then has, we do not even give the name of life. It is then only when a man is born, that we say he begins to live. For as soon as he is born, he begins to see the light, and the various objects with which he is encompassed. His ears are then opened, and he hears the sounds which successively strike upon them. At the same time, all the other organs of sense begin to be exercised upon their proper objects. He likewise breathes, and lives in a manner wholly different from what he did before. How exactly doth the parallel hold in all these instances? While a man is in a mere natural state, before he is born of God, he has in a spiritual sense, eyes and sees not; a thick impenetrable veil lies upon them; he has ears, but hears not; he is utterly deaf to what he is most of all concerned to hear. His other spiritual senses are all locked up;

he is in the same condition as if he had them not. Hence he has no knowledge of God; no intercourse with him; he is not at all acquainted with him. He has no true knowledge of the things of God, either of spiritual or eternal things; therefore, though he is a living man, he is a dead Christian. But as soon as he is born of God, there is a total change in all these particulars. The 'eyes of his understanding are opened' ... and he who of old 'commanded light to shine out of darkness' shining on his heart, he sees the light of the glory of God, his glorious love, 'in the face of Jesus Christ'. His ears being opened, he is now capable of hearing the inward voice of God, saying 'Be of good cheer, thy sins are forgiven thee' and 'Go and sin no more.' ... He feels 'the love of God shed abroad in his heart by the Holy Ghost which is given unto him'; and all his spiritual senses are then exercised to discern spiritual good and evil ... And now he may be properly said to live: God having quickened him by his Spirit, he is alive to God through Jesus Christ.

I rode to a neighbouring town, to wait upon a justice of peace, a man of candour and understanding; before whom (I was informed) their angry neighbours had carried a whole waggon-load of these new heretics. But when he asked what they had done there was a deep silence; for that was a point their conductors had forgot. At length one said, 'Why, they pretended to be better than other people; and besides, they prayed from morning to night.' Mr S. asked, 'But have they done nothing besides?' 'Yes, sir,' said an old man, 'an't please your worship, they have converted my wife. Till she went among them, she had such a tongue! And now she is as quiet as a lamb.' 'Carry them back, carry them back,' replied the justice, 'and let them convert all the scolds in the town.'

FROM THE 'JOURNAL'

John Wesley preached his last open-air sermon under this tree
at Winchelsea in the south of England in 1790, at the age of
eighty-seven.

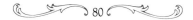

DAVID BRAINERD

1718–1747

Brainerd's *Journal* has inspired more Christians to
become missionaries than any book other than the Bible. Born
near Hartford, Connecticut, and orphaned at fourteen, Brainerd
was a pious young man who, on his own confession, 'had a very
good outside, and rested entirely on my duties'. It was only
when he realized his powerlessness to earn his salvation that God
became real to him.

Expelled from Yale for an ill-advised remark about a
professor, he offered himself for missionary service. He was sent to
the American Indians with a licence to preach but was given no
training and had no knowledge of their language. Once he
preached through an interpreter who was so drunk he could hardly
stand. Yet through Brainerd's sincerity and commitment—he would
spend whole days in prayer—even that sermon converted
thousands. He died at twenty-nine, only a short time after seeing
the first fruits of his work. The longer-term fruits came after his
death and were seen in the lives of great Christians such as John
Wesley, Jonathan Edwards, William Carey and Henry Martyn who,
having read the *Journal*, felt compelled to spend their lives
preaching the gospel.

THE 'AWAKENING' AMONGST THE INDIANS

In the afternoon I preached to the Indians
upon Luke 15:16–23. There was much
visible concern among them, while I was
discoursing publicly; but afterwards, when
I spoke to one and another more particularly, whom I perceived under much
concern, the power of God seemed to
descend upon the assembly 'like a mighty
rushing wind', and with an astonishing
energy bore down all before it.

I stood amazed at the influence, which
seized the audience almost universally; and
could compare it to nothing more aptly
than the irresistible force of a mighty
torrent, or a swelling deluge, that with its
insupportable weight and pressure bears
down and sweeps before it whatever comes
in its way.

Almost all persons of all ages were
bowed down with concern together, and
scarcely one was able to withstand the
shock of this surprising operation. They
were almost universally praying and crying
for mercy in every part of the house, and

many were out of doors; and numbers
could neither go nor stand . . .

Some of the white people who came out
of curiosity to hear what 'this babbler'
would say to the poor ignorant Indians
were much awakened; and some appeared
to be wounded with a view of their
perishing state. Those who had lately
obtained relief, were filled with comfort at
this season. They appeared calm and
composed, and seemed to rejoice in Christ
Jesus. Some of them took their distressed
friends by the hand, telling them of the
goodness of Christ, and the comfort that is
to be enjoyed in him; and thence invited
them to come and give up their hearts to
him . . .

It is remarkable that God began this
work among the Indians at a time when I
had the least hope and, to my apprehension, the least rational prospect, of seeing a
work of grace propagated amongst them.
My hopes respecting the conversion of the
Indians were perhaps never reduced to so

low an ebb, since I had any special concern for them, as at this time. Yet this was the very season in which God saw fit to begin this glorious work! . . .

This great awakening, this surprising concern, was never excited by harangues of terror, but always appeared most remarkable when I insisted upon the compassion of a dying Saviour, the plentiful provisions of the gospel, and the free offers of divine grace to needy, distressed sinners . . .

If ever my soul presented itself to God for his service, without any reserve, it did so now. The language of my thoughts and disposition now was, 'Here I am, Lord, send me; send me to the ends of the earth; send me to the rough, the savage pagans of the wilderness; send me from all that is called comfort in earth . . . send me even to death itself; if it be but in thy service and to promote thy Kingdom.'

David Brainerd's *Journal*, recording his outreach to the Indians, inspired many to become missionaries. This illustration is of John Eliot who pioneered work among the Indians.

WILLIAM CAREY

1761–1834

'Sit down, young man; when God wants to convert the heathen, he'll do it without your help or mine', said a minister when Carey spoke on overseas missions at a local Baptist meeting. But Carey would not accept such complacency. Converted himself through the witness of a fellow apprentice shoemaker, he believed passionately in Christ's call to 'preach the gospel to all nations'. In the spring of 1792 he published a slim booklet called *An Enquiry into the Obligation of Christians to use Means for the Conversion of the Heathen*. Shortly afterwards, in Nottingham, he preached a famous sermon in which he called Christians to 'Expect great things from God; attempt great things for God.' The impact of both book and sermon was enormous. Within months the Baptist Missionary Society was formed, and a host of others of all denominations soon followed.

Carey himself left his job as pastor of a Leicester Baptist church to serve as a missionary in India. There he studied and taught Indian languages, supervised nearly thirty Bible translations, founded schools and colleges, promoted agricultural development and campaigned for the abolition of widow-burning. He was also far ahead of his time in encouraging the training of local converts, and in boycotting products such as Caribbean rum and sugar obtained by slave labour.

William Carey realized that education could be used to win converts and train them to evangelize their own country. He founded schools and colleges and translated the Bible into several Oriental languages.

PORTRAIT OF A MISSIONARY

The missionaries must be men of great piety, prudence, courage, and forbearance; of undoubted orthodoxy in their sentiments, and must enter with all their hearts into the spirit of their mission; they must be willing to leave all the comforts of life behind them, and to encounter all the hardships of a torrid or a frigid climate, an uncomfortable manner of living, and every other inconvenience that can attend this undertaking. Clothing, a few knives, powder and shot, fishing-tackle, and the articles of husbandry above mentioned, must be provided for them; and when

arrived at the place of their destination, their first business must be to gain some acquaintance with the language of the natives (for which purpose two would be better than one), and by all lawful means to endeavour to cultivate a friendship with them, and as soon as possible let them know the errand for which they were sent. They must endeavour to convince them that it was their good alone which induced them to forsake their friends, and all the comforts of their native country. They must be very careful not to resent injuries which may be offered to them, nor to think highly of themselves, so as to despise the poor heathens, and by those means lay a foundation for their resentment, or rejection of the gospel. They must take every opportunity of doing them good, and labouring, and travelling, night and day,

CHARLES FINNEY
1792–1875

Finney, a young law student in New York State, was converted through being taken to services by a friend. Almost immediately he gave up his studies and began to preach, saying he had been given 'a retainer from the Lord to plead his cause'. He was ordained as a Presbyterian minister in 1824, and spent eight years conducting revivals in the eastern states, with spectacular results.

During that time he delivered a series of lectures on how revivals happen. They were published in 1835 and the book became an instant best seller. That same year Finney became a professor of theology at Oberlin College, Ohio, where he would later be president. But he continued to be active as an evangelist, and even made two tours of Britain in the 1850s and 60s.

With no theological training, indeed little formal education of any kind, Finney nevertheless became a major influence on the course of religion in America. He was committed to social reform, particularly the anti-slavery movement and the temperance movement. One of his campaigns was against tea and coffee, which he considered unnecessary stimulants and a waste of money which could be used for God's work!

LONG PRAYERS IN MEETINGS

Commonly, those who pray long in a meeting do so, not because they have the spirit of prayer, but because they have not. Some men will spin out a long prayer in telling God who and what he is, or they pray out a whole system of divinity. Some they must instruct, exhort, and rebuke, with all long-suffering and anxious desire for them, and, above all, must be instant in prayer for the effusion of the Holy Spirit upon the people of their charge. Let but missionaries of the above description engage in the work, and we shall see that it is not impracticable.

preach; others exhort the people—till everybody wishes they would stop and God wishes so too, most undoubtedly. They should keep to the point, and pray for what they came to pray for, and not follow the imagination of their own hearts all over the universe.

———— FROM 'LECTURES ON REVIVALS ———— OF RELIGION'

TEACHING YOUNG CONVERTS

One of the first things young converts should be taught is to distinguish between emotion and principle in religion . . . When a man is fully determined to obey God, because it is *right* that he should obey God, I call that principle . . . Many young converts . . . depend almost entirely on the state of their feelings to go forward in duty. Some will not lead a prayer-meeting, unless they feel as if they could make an eloquent prayer . . . Young converts should be carefully taught that when duty is before them they are to *do it* . . . Do not wait for feeling, but *do it*! Most likely the very emotions for which you would wait, will be called into the exercise when you begin to do your duty . . .

Young converts should not be made sectarian in their feelings. They should not be taught to dwell on sectarian distinctions, or to be sticklish about sectarian points. They ought to examine these points, according to their importance, at a proper time, and in a proper way, and make up their minds for themselves. But they should not be taught to dwell on them, or to make much of them at the outset of the religious life.

When I hear them asking, 'Do you believe in the doctrine of Election?', or, 'Do you believe in sprinkling?', or, 'Do you believe in immersing?', I feel sad. I never knew such converts to be worth much.

———— FROM 'LECTURES ON REVIVALS OF RELIGION' ————

SØREN KIERKEGAARD
1813–1855

Kierkegaard's parents were well into middle age when Søren, their seventh child, was born. His wealthy father's rather severe piety dominated the family: 'We heard more of the Crucified and the martyrs than of the Christ-child and good angels.'

Teased at school for his slight spinal deformity and his old-fashioned clothes, Søren developed a brilliant and biting wit. After studying theology, he became a leading light of Copenhagen's café society, writing on a wide range of subjects under such pen names as Hilarius Bookbinder and Frater Taciturnus. But the jokes hid a constant depression which led him to break his engagement for his fiancée's sake. Other troubles included frequent debts and a long-running feud with a magazine called *Corsair*.

In his religious writings such as *Fear and Trembling* and *Repetition*, Kierkegaard explored difficult biblical stories, for instance, Abraham's sacrifice of Isaac or the sufferings of Job. His belief that faith could only be reached by 'a leap in the dark' was an important influence on the twentieth-century existentialists. He hated organized religion, seeing himself as a 'spy of the Most High' whose mission was 'to reintroduce Christianity to Christendom'.

COMPLAINING TO GOD

Nowadays people are of the opinion that the natural expression of sorrow, the desperate language of passion, must be left to poets, who as attorneys in a lower court plead the sufferer's cause before the tribunal of human compassion. Further than this no one ventures to go. Speak therefore, O Job of imperishable memory! Rehearse everything thou didst say, thou mighty advocate who dost confront the highest tribunal, no more daunted than a roaring lion! ... Thee I have need of, a man who knows how to complain aloud, so that his complaint echoes in heaven where God confers with Satan in devising schemes against a man.

Complain! The Lord is not afraid, he is well able to defend himself, but how might he be able to speak in his defence if no one ventures to complain as it is seemly for a man to do? Speak, lift up thy voice, speak aloud, God surely can speak louder, he possesses the thunder—but that too is an answer, an explanation, reliable, trust-worthy, genuine, an answer from God himself, an answer which even if it crush a man is more glorious than gossip and rumour about the righteousness of providence which are invented by human wisdom ...

FROM 'REPETITION'

THE PARABLE OF THE GEESE

Try to imagine for a moment that geese could talk—that they had so arranged things that they too had their divine service, their worship of God. Every Sunday they would meet and listen to the gander's sermon. The gander would dwell on the glorious destiny of geese, the high goal for which their maker had created them—and every time his name was mentioned all the geese would curtsey and the ganders bow their heads. They were to use their wings to fly away to distant lands, blissful regions, where they truly belonged, for they were only strangers on this earth.

It was the same every Sunday. When the service was over the congregation would rise and they would all waddle home. And the next Sunday they would meet for worship again, and go home again—but that was as far as they ever got. They would thrive and grow fat, plump and tasty, and at Martinmas they would be eaten—and that would be that . . . For while their conversation on Sundays was very impressive, on Mondays they would tell each other about what had happened to a goose who tried in earnest to use the wings the Creator had given it to reach the high goal set before it—what terrible things it had had to endure. All this was of course common knowledge among the geese, but naturally no one mentioned the subject on Sundays, for, as they said, it would then become obvious that to attend the service was a mockery both of God and of themselves.

Among the geese were several who looked pale and were losing weight, and all the other geese said, 'There—you see what comes of taking flying seriously. It is all because they can't think of anything but flying that they lose weight and grow pale and don't enjoy God's blessings like we do—for that's what makes us plump and tasty.'

And next Sunday they would go to church again, and the old gander would preach about the glorious end for which the Creator (and here all the geese would curtsey and the ganders bow their heads) had destined them, for which he had given them their wings.

And it's just the same with divine worship in Christianity . . .

FROM KIERKEGAARD'S DIARY

Kierkegaard lived and wrote in Copenhagen. But his work was not fully appreciated until after his death. He is now acknowledged as one of the greatest influences on twentieth-century philosophy.

GEORGE MACDONALD

1824–1905

'The most Christlike man of letters of his day,' was a contemporary's view of MacDonald. The son of a poor Aberdeenshire weaver, George spent his childhood in a cottage so small he had to sleep in the attic. It was a happy time, full of simple pleasures which he later described in several novels of Scottish rural life.

After studying at Aberdeen University, George trained for the ministry in London and became the minister of the Congregational church in Arundel, Sussex. But owing to theological disagreements, the deacons lowered his salary to force him to leave. A second pastorate in Manchester was also short-lived, and George decided to devote himself to writing. He took his growing family back to London, where their constant poverty was relieved by help from Lord Byron's widow. A lively literary circle which included Lewis Carroll and Lord Tennyson gathered in their home, 'The Retreat'.

MacDonald's most popular novels, such as *Phantastes* and *Lilith* for adults, and the *The Princess and the Goblin* for children, are fairy stories in which spiritual realities break through into everyday life, often through mysterious 'fairy godmother' figures. *At the Back of the North Wind*, set in Victorian London, tells the story of how the little cab-driver's son Diamond meets North Wind and learns from her the meaning of suffering. Stories like these were a major influence on later writers such as J. R. R. Tolkien and C. S. Lewis, who said, 'I regard MacDonald as my master.'

CURDIE'S HANDS

Curdie dared not stop to think. It was much too terrible to think about. He rushed to the fire, and thrust both of his hands right into the middle of the heap of flaming roses, and his arms halfway up to the elbows. And it *did* hurt! . . . At last it ceased altogether, and Curdie thought his hands must be burned to cinders if not ashes, for he did not feel them at all. The princess told him to take them out and look at them. He did so, and found that all that was gone of them was the rough, hard

An illustration from
a first edition of George MacDonald's
The Light Princess, a collection
of short fantasy stories.

skin; they were white and smooth like the princess's.

'Come to me,' she said . . . 'Would you like to know why I made you put your hands in the fire?'

Curdie looked at them again—then said:

'To take the marks of the work off them and make them fit for the king's court, I suppose.'

'No, Curdie,' answered the princess . . . 'It would be a poor way of making your hands fit for the king's court to take off them signs of his service. There is a far greater difference on them than that . . . Have you ever heard what some philosophers say—that men were all animals once?'

'No, ma'am.'

'It is of no consequence. But there is another thing that is of the greatest consequence—this: that all men, if they do not take care, go down hill to the animals' country; that many men are actually, all their lives, going to be beasts. People knew it once, but it is long since they forgot it . . . Now listen. Since it is always what they *do*, whether in their minds or their bodies, that makes men go down to be less than men, that is, beasts, the change always comes first in their hands—and first of all in the inside hands, to which the outside ones are but as the gloves . . . Now here is what the rosefire has done for you: it has made your hands so knowing and wise, it has brought your real hands so near the outside of your flesh gloves that you will henceforth be able to know at once the hand of a man who is growing into a beast; nay, more— you will at once feel the foot of the beast he is growing, just as if there were no glove made like a man's hand between you and it.'

FROM 'THE PRINCESS AND CURDIE'

GOODNESS AND BEAUTY

'Well, please, North Wind, you are so beautiful, I am quite ready to go with you.'

'You must not be ready to go with everything beautiful all at once, Diamond.'

'But what's beautiful can't be bad. You're not bad, North Wind?'

'No; I'm not bad. But sometimes beautiful things grow bad by doing bad, and it takes some time for their badness to spoil their beauty. So little boys may be mistaken if they go after things because they are beautiful.'

'Well, I will go with you because you are beautiful and good too.'

'Ah, but there's another thing too, Diamond; what if I should look ugly without being bad—look ugly myself because I am making ugly things beautiful? What then?'

'I don't quite understand you, North Wind. You tell me what then.'

'Well, I will tell you. If you see me with my face all black, don't be frightened. If you see me flapping wings like a bat's, as big as the whole sky, don't be frightened. If you hear me raging ten times worse than Mrs Bill, the blacksmith's wife—even if you see me looking in at windows like Mrs Eve Dropper, the gardener's wife—you must believe that I am doing my work. Nay, Diamond, if I change into a serpent or a tiger, you must not let go your hold of me, for my hand will never change in yours if you keep a good hold. If you keep a hold, you will know who I am all the time, even when you look at me and can't see me the least like the North Wind. I may look something very awful. Do you understand?'

'Quite well,' said little Diamond.

'Come along, then,' said North Wind.

FROM 'AT THE BACK OF THE NORTH WIND'

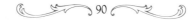

LEO TOLSTOY

1828–1910

In the late 1870s Count Leo Nikolaevich Tolstoy was at the height of his career as a novelist. The Napoleonic epic *War and Peace* and the tragic love story *Anna Karenina* had made him famous all over the world. But Tolstoy was unhappy with the comfortable lifestyle which his inherited wealth had always allowed him to enjoy. Already, in 1861, he had freed his serfs, and now he decided to take a much more revolutionary step. He disclaimed his title and the copyrights of his books, shared out his estate among his wife and nine children, and threw in his lot with the peasants, living and working exactly as they did.

His reasons for this drastic change are outlined in *My Religion* (also known as 'What I Believe' and 'Confession'), published in 1882. The key text of his life was 'Do not resist an evil person; but if someone strikes you on the right cheek, turn to him the other also.' This, to him, summed up what Christ taught.

THE REGULATIONS

The other day I happened to walk through the Borovitsky Gate (in Moscow). In the gateway sat an old and crippled beggar with his head wrapped in a rag. I took out my purse to give him a trifle. At that moment a smart-looking, ruddy young fellow, in a grenadier's uniform, came running down from the Kremlin. On seeing him the beggar started up in a fright, and hobbled away as fast as he could down towards the Alexander Garden. The grenadier gave chase, but, not gaining on him, stopped, and abused him with shouts for having broken the regulations by sitting in the gateway. I waited for the grenadier, and when he came up, asked if he had learnt to read.

'Yes, I have. What then?'

'Have you read the Gospel?'

'I have.'

'Well, have you read the passage, "And he who feeds the hungry . . ."?' And I quoted the words.

He knew it, and listened to me. I saw that he was puzzled. Two passers-by stopped to listen. The grenadier evidently felt it rather hard that, when he had done his duty well by driving people away according to his orders, he should suddenly appear to be in the wrong. He was confused, and was evidently seeking for an excuse. Suddenly a light shone in his intelligent black eyes; he turned away from me as if going. 'And have you read the military regulations?'

I answered that I had not done so.

'Then hold your tongue!' said he, shaking his head triumphantly, as, wrapping his fur coat round him, he stalked proudly to his post.

This was the only man I had ever met in my life who with strict logic had decided the eternal question which, in our actual social state, lay before me, and lies before every man calling himself a Christian.

FROM 'MY RELIGION'

WILLIAM BOOTH
1829–1912

'My ambition is the souls of men' wrote Booth in King
Edward VII's autograph book in 1904. At heart an evangelist,
Booth was unable to persuade the Methodist church, which by the
mid-nineteenth century had become staid and respectable, to
support his travelling ministry. So in 1865 he and his remarkable
wife Catherine began the independent Christian Mission in a tent
in London's East End. 'We can't get at the masses in the chapels,'
said Catherine.
Within a few years the mission had become the
'Salvation Army', with its own uniform, officers and military-style
bands. Their methods of 'getting at the masses' were often
unorthodox, and even the aged evangelical reformer Lord Shaftes-
bury concluded that the Army was a trick of the devil to make
Christianity ridiculous! But the Army's style worked,
and thousands were converted.
As they made contact with some of the most destitute,
the Booths became more and more concerned to change the social
conditions which caused such human misery. In 1890 William
published *In Darkest England and the Way Out*, in which he sought
to show that the poorest ten per cent in Britain were as needy as
the slaves in 'darkest Africa'. The book outlined an ambitious
programme of urban and rural 'settlements' to provide work and
housing. Today the Army Booth founded has centres in a total of
eighty-seven countries.

THE SEA AND THE ROCK

I saw a dark and stormy ocean. Over it the
black clouds hung heavily; through them
every now and then vivid lightnings
flashed and loud thunders rolled, while the
winds moaned, and the waves rose and
foamed and fretted and broke and rose to
foam and fret and break again.

In that ocean I thought I saw myriads of
poor human beings plunging and floating,
shouting and shrieking, cursing and struggling and drowning; and as they cursed
and shrieked, they rose and shrieked again,
and then sank to rise no more.

And out of this dark angry ocean I saw a
mighty rock that rose up with its summit
towering high above the black clouds that
overhung the stormy sea; and all round the
base of this rock I saw a vast platform; and
on this platform I saw with delight a
number of the poor, struggling, drowning
wretches continually climbing out of the
angry ocean; and I saw that a number of
those who were already safe on the platform were helping the poor creatures still in
the angry waters to reach the same place of
safety . . .

And as I looked I saw that the occu-
pants of that platform were quite a mixed
company. That is, they were divided into
different 'sets' or castes and occupied themselves with different pleasures and employ-
ments; but only a very few of them seemed
to make it their business to get the people
out of the sea . . . Some of them were
absorbed night and day in trading, in order
to make gain, storing up their savings in
boxes, strong rooms and the like . . . Many
spent their time in amusing themselves

with growing flowers on the side of the rock; others in painting pieces of cloth, or in playing music, or in dressing themselves up in different styles and walking about to be admired.

Some occupied themselves chiefly in eating and drinking, others were greatly taken up with arguing about the poor drowning creatures in the sea and as to what would become of them in the future, while many contented themselves that they did their duty to the perishing creatures by the performance of curious religious ceremonies . . .

And all this time the struggling, shrieking multitudes were floating about in the dark sea, quite near by—so near that they could easily have been rescued.

------- FROM 'IN DARKEST ENGLAND AND THE WAY OUT' -------

THE 'CAB-HORSE CHARTER'

I sorrowfully admit that it would be utopian in our present social arrangements to dream of attaining for every honest Englishman a jail standard of all the necessaries of life. Some time, perhaps, we may venture to hope that every honest worker on English soil will always be as warmly clad, as healthily housed, and as regularly fed as our criminal convicts—but that is not yet . . .

What, then, is the standard towards which we may venture to aim with some prospect of realization in our time? It is a very humble one, but if realized it would solve the worst problems of modern society. It is the standard of the London cab horse.

When in the streets of London a cab horse, weary or careless or stupid, trips and falls and lies stretched out in the midst of the traffic, there is no question of debating how he came to stumble before we try to get him on his legs again. The cab horse is a very real illustration of poor, broken-down humanity; he usually falls down because of overwork and underfeeding. If you put him on his feet again without altering his conditions, it would only be to give him another dose of agony; but first of all you'll have to pick him up again . . . That is the first point. The second is that every cab horse in London has three things: a shelter for the night, food for its stomach, and work allotted to it by which it can earn its corn.

These are the two points of the Cab-horse Charter. When he is down he is helped up, and while he lives he has food, shelter and work. That, although a humble standard, is at present absolutely unattainable by millions—literally by millions—of our fellow men and women in this country. Can the Cab-horse charter be gained for human beings? I answer, yes.

------- FROM 'IN DARKEST ENGLAND AND THE WAY OUT' -------

William Booth preaching to a crowd in London's East End in 1865. Concern for their extreme poverty led him to combine evangelism with an attack on social evils.

HANNAH WHITALL SMITH

1832–1911

The daughter of a pious Philadelphia Quaker family, Hannah Whitall suffered from depression and doubt in her adolescence which lasted until she came to faith through contact with the Brethren movement in 1858. Robert Pearsall Smith was converted through the Presbyterian church that same year, and soon the two were to meet and marry. In 1867 Hannah gained a new understanding of spiritual victory, from the promise found in the book of Romans 'that we should no longer be slaves to sin'. She and Robert organized a series of interdenominational meetings on 'the higher Christian life', teaching that Christians should experience greater victory over sin.

In 1872 the Smiths had to move to Britain for Robert's health. They continued the meetings there, with phenomenal success. A few years later Hannah's book *The Christian's Secret of a Happy Life* was published. The popularity of the book and the meetings contributed greatly to the founding and development of the Keswick Convention, an annual 'teach-in' on holiness of life, which still continues today.

—WHAT FAITH REALLY IS—

Your idea of faith, I suppose, has been something like this. You have looked upon it as in some way a sort of *thing*—either a religious exercise of soul, or an inward, gracious disposition of heart; something tangible, in fact, which, when you have secured it, you can look at and rejoice over, and use as a passport to God's favour, or a coin with which to purchase his gifts. And you have been praying for faith, expecting all the while to get something like this; and never having received any such thing, you are insisting upon it that you have no faith. Now faith, in fact, is not in the least like this. It is nothing at all tangible. It is simply believing God; and, like sight, it is nothing apart from its object. You might as well shut your eyes and look inside to see whether you have sight, as to look inside to discover whether you have faith. You see

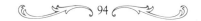

something, and thus know that you have sight; you believe something, and thus know that you have faith. For as sight is only seeing, so faith is only believing. And as the only necessary thing about sight is that you see the thing as it is, so the only necessary thing about faith is that you believe the thing as it is. The virtue does not lie in your believing, but in the thing you believe.

FREE FORGIVENESS

Our feeling is that it is presumptuous, and even almost impertinent, to go at once to the Lord, after having sinned against him. It seems as if we ought to suffer the consequences of our sin first for a little while, and endure the accusings of our conscience; and we can hardly believe that the Lord *can* be willing at once to receive us back into loving fellowship with himself.

A little girl once expressed this feeling to me, with a child's outspoken candour. She had asked whether the Lord Jesus always forgave us for our sins as soon as we asked him, and I had said, 'Yes, of course he does.' '*Just* as soon?' she repeated doubtingly. 'Yes,' I replied, 'the very minute we ask, he forgives us.' 'Well,' she said deliberately, 'I cannot believe that. I should think he would make us feel sorry for two or three days first. And then I should think he would make us ask him a great many times, and in a very pretty way too, not just in common talk. And I believe that *is* the way he does, and you need not try to make me think he forgives me right at once, no matter what the Bible says.' She only *said* what most Christians *think*, and what is worse, what most Christians act on, making their discouragement and their remorse separate them infinitely further off from God than their sin would have done.

CHARLES HADDON SPURGEON

1834–1892

The son and grandson of Independent ministers,
Spurgeon was coverted through hearing a sermon in a Methodist
church where he was sheltering from a snowstorm. He became
pastor of a Cambridgeshire village Baptist church, and by his
twentieth birthday was in charge of a large chapel in Southwark,
South London. His humour, directness and command of everyday
language soon brought him fame as a preacher. In 1861 the huge
Metropolitan Tabernacle, seating 6,000, was built specially to
accommodate the vast crowds who came to hear him. Here he was
to preach for the next thirty years.

Spurgeon was involved in many enterprises. Among
them was a society for distributing Christian literature, a monthly
magazine called *The Sword and the Trowel*, designed to promote
practical Christian living, an orphanage, and a pastors' training
college which he funded entirely out of his own pocket for its first
fifteen years. Spurgeon's favourite reading matter was the work of
the seventeenth-century Puritans, and he fought often bitter battles
against the gradual 'watering down' of Christian doctrine in the
late ninetenth century. His sermons were published weekly and sold
in great numbers. It is estimated that his preaching brought nearly
15,000 new members into the church.

————————GOD JUDGES DIFFERENTLY————————

How often have I thought, 'There is a
young woman in the gallery, or a young
man; how interested they look during the
sermon!' I have met with them, I have
admired their characters; they have had an
amiable carriage and deportment; there
has been much in them that everybody
would tell others to imitate and emulate. I
have said, 'Ah! I shall soon have them
added to the church; there is so much good
about them, it will be such an easy tran-
sition for them; they are so moral and
excellent it will be very easy for them surely
to take a step into the kingdom of heaven.'
I don't say I have said so in words to my
heart, but that has been about what I have
thought. Well, there has been a fellow who
came into chapel one evening, a queer
looking object certainly; he came running
in one Thursday evening towards the end
of the service, not washed or anything; he
only just came to hear something that
would make him laugh as he thought. I did
not expect to see him converted. The next
time I sat to hear inquiries, in he came,
cleaned and washed a bit; but I recognized
him for all that and I said to him, 'Didn't
you come in one Thursday night after you
had been hammering and tinkering somewhere? I thought you looked a strange one,
certainly.' 'Yes,' said he, 'and the Lord met
with me.' Now, I sat many and many a

night, and I did not see the young man or the young woman come . . .

Then, again, we have sometimes said, 'If such a one were converted, dear me, what a shining Christian he would make! He is a man of brilliant talent, of great intellectual power, and of extensive fortune. Oh if he were converted, what a jubilee it would be to the church of God! How much he would do!' Well, do you know, I have always found that these fine people, who when they were converted were to be somebody, if they have been converted and we have got them, have not turned out to be quite so great after all!

———— FROM A SERMON ————

For a while Spurgeon was pastor of New Park Street Chapel, Southwark, London (above). Soon his preaching attracted such a large congregation that it became necessary to build the much larger Metropolitan Tabernacle.

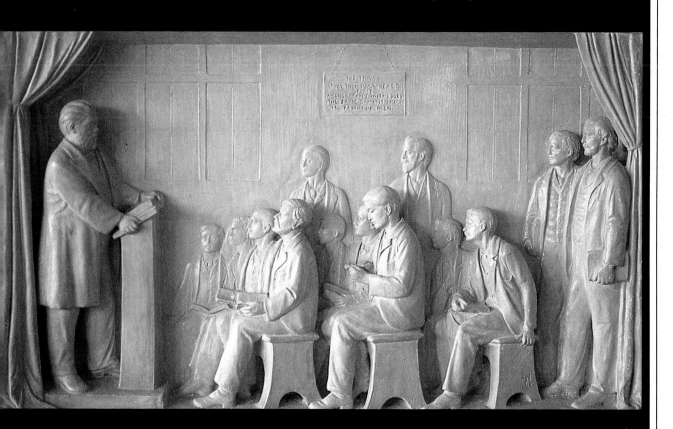

Spurgeon was anxious to train others for the ministry and founded a Pastors' College in 1856.

KARL BARTH

1886–1968

In 1914, at the start of World War I, a group of German
university lecturers, including theologians, published a statement
supporting Kaiser Wilhelm II's policies. Karl Barth, the son of a
Swiss theology professor and himself a theologian, was profoundly
shocked. 'So far as I was concerned', he wrote later, 'there was no
more future for the theology of the nineteenth century.' An
optimistic belief in man's progress, fuelled by Darwin's theory of
evolution, had ended in support for a brutal and unnecessary war.

From then on Barth's views showed his acceptance of
the biblical picture of man's fallenness and inability to reach God.
The key to his teaching is found in his biblical commentary, *The
Epistle to the Romans*, published in 1919. Only God's revelation
in Christ, he argued, can break through the futility of our efforts
to save ourselves.

It was Barth's thinking which helped form the famous
Barmen Declaration of 1934, opposing National Socialism, and
later to inspire the Confessing Church in Nazi Germany. In 1935
Barth refused to swear allegiance to Hitler; he was sacked from his
university post and exiled. In Switzerland he continued to teach
and to write his *Church Dogmatics*, a work which, though
unfinished, has been compared for its breadth and scope to Thomas
Aquinas' *Summa Theologiae*.

SAVED BY GRACE

Someone once said to me, 'I need not go to church. I need not read the Bible. I know already what the church teaches and what the Bible says: "Do what is right and fear no one!"' Let me say this at this point: if this were the message at stake, I would most certainly not have come here. My time is too precious and so is yours. To say that, neither prophets nor apostles, neither Bible, Jesus Christ nor God are needed. Anybody is at liberty to say this to himself. By the same token this saying is void of any new, of any very special and exciting message. It does not help anyone. I have never seen a smile on the face of a person reassuring himself with this kind of talk . . . Let us hear therefore what the Bible says and what we as Christians are called to hear together: By grace you have been

saved! No man can say this to himself. Neither can he say it to someone else. This can only be said by God to each one of us. It takes Jesus Christ to make this saying true . . .

You probably all know the legend of the rider who crossed the frozen Lake of Constance by night without knowing it. When he reached the opposite shore and was told whence he came, he broke down, horrified. This is the human situation when the sky opens and the earth is bright, when we may hear: By grace you have been saved! In such a moment we are like that terrified rider. When we hear this word we involuntarily look back, do we not, asking ourselves: Where have I been? Over an abyss, in mortal danger! What did I do? The most foolish thing I ever attempted!

What happened? I was doomed and miraculously escaped and now I am safe! . . .

Look once again to Jesus Christ in his death upon the cross. Look and try to understand that what he did and suffered he did and suffered for you, for me, for us all. He carried our sin, our captivity and our suffering, and did not carry it in vain. *He carried it away*. He acted as the captain of us all. He broke through the ranks of our enemies. He has already won the battle, our battle. All we have to do is to follow him, to be victorious with him. Through him, in him we are saved. Our sin no longer has any power over us. Our prison door is open . . . When he, the Son of God, sets us free, we are *truly* free.

FROM 'DELIVERANCE TO THE CAPTIVES'

C. S. Lewis

1898–1963

It was on the top of an English double-decker bus that a long intellectual battle ended and Clive Staples Lewis gave in to Christ—'perhaps', in his own words, 'the most dejected and reluctant convert in history.'

Lewis' motherless childhood in Belfast was an emotionally austere one; and he hated his time at Malvern School. He retreated into the world of fairy-tale and Norse mythology, which was later to inspire his many fictional writings. Under the influence of an atheist tutor he abandoned his childhood faith. He was not to regain it until his early thirties, by which time he had begun a brilliant academic career in the department of English Literature at Oxford. After his conversion he poured out a stream of writings of every type—from literary criticism and linguistic scholarship to popular defences of Christianity and allegorical novels for adults and children. Among the most popular are the 'Narnia' series of children's stories, the autobiography *Surprised by Joy*, the highly readable *Mere Christianity*, and *The Screwtape Letters*, in which a senior devil advises a junior on how to keep a 'patient' from 'the Enemy', in other words, God. In all Lewis' writings absolute clarity of thought combines with warm humour and imaginative illustrations. 'Lewis possesses the rare gift of making righteousness readable,' said the atheist philosopher C. M. Joad.

——BEYOND DEFINITION——

'In our world,' said Eustace, 'a star is a huge ball of flaming gas.'

'Even in your world, my son, that is not what a star is but only what it is made of.'

———— FROM 'THE VOYAGE OF THE ———— DAWN TREADER'

——MAD, BAD OR GOD——

'I'm ready to accept Jesus as a great moral teacher, but I don't accept his claim to be God.' That is the one thing we must not say. A man who was merely a man and said the sort of things Jesus said would not be a great moral teacher. He would be either a lunatic—on a level with the man who says he is a poached egg—or else he would be the Devil of Hell. You must make your choice. Either this man was, and is, the Son of God; or else a madman or something worse. You can shut him up for a fool, you can spit at him and kill him as a demon, or you can fall at his feet and call him Lord and God. But let us not come with any patronizing nonsense about his being a great human teacher. He has not left that open to us. He did not intend to.

——————FROM 'MERE CHRISTIANITY'——————

C. S. Lewis loved the British countryside. From it he drew images which later appeared in his writings. In 1930 he walked with three friends from Dunster to Challacombe in south-west England, a journey which took them along the valley of the River Lynn.

CHRIST THE LION

'Are you not thirsty?' said the Lion.

'I'm *dying* of thirst,' said Jill.

'Then drink,' said the Lion.

'May I—could I—would you mind going away while I do?' said Jill.

The Lion answered this only by a look and a very low growl . . .

'I daren't come and drink,' said Jill.

'Then you will die of thirst,' said the Lion.

'Oh dear!' said Jill, coming another step nearer. 'I suppose I must go and look for another stream then.'

'There is no other stream,' said the Lion.

———— FROM 'THE SILVER CHAIR' ————

A DEVIL'S EYE VIEW OF THE CHURCH

My dear Wormwood,

I notice with grave displeasure that your patient has become a Christian . . . There is no need to despair; hundreds of these adult converts have been reclaimed after a brief sojourn in the Enemy's camp and are now with us. All the *habits* of the patient, both mental and bodily, are still in our favour.

One of our great allies at present is the Church itself. Do not misunderstand me. I do not mean the Church as we see her spread out through all time and space and rooted in eternity, terrible as an army with banners. That, I confess, is a spectacle which makes our boldest tempters uneasy. But fortunately it is quite invisible to these humans. All your patient sees is the half-finished, sham Gothic erection on the new building estate. When he goes inside, he sees the local grocer with rather an oily expression on his face bustling up to offer him one shiny little book containing a liturgy which neither of them understand and one shabby little book containing corrupt texts of a number of religious lyrics, mostly bad, and in very small print. When he gets to his pew and looks round him he sees just that selection of his neighbours whom he has hitherto avoided. You want to lean pretty heavily on those neighbours. Make his mind flit to and fro between an expression like 'the body of Christ' and the actual faces in the next pew. It matters very little, of course, what kind of people the next pew really contains. You may know one of them to be a great warrior on the Enemy's side. No matter . . . Provided that any of those neighbours sing out of tune, or have boots that squeak, or double chins, or odd clothes, the patient will quite easily believe that their religion must therefore be somehow ridiculous.

———— FROM 'THE SCREWTAPE LETTERS' ————

'Suppose we *have* only dreamed, or made up, all those things—trees and grass and sun and moon and stars and Aslan himself. Suppose we have. Then all I can say is that, in that case, the made-up things seem a good deal more important than the real ones. Suppose this black pit of a kingdom of yours *is* the only world. Well, it strikes me as a pretty poor one. And that's a funny thing, when you come to think of it. We're just babies making up a game, if you're right. But four babies playing a game can make a play-world which licks your real world hollow. That's why I'm going to stand by the play world. I'm on Aslan's side even if there isn't any Aslan to lead it. I'm going to live as like a Narnian as I can even if there isn't any Narnia.'

FROM 'THE SILVER CHAIR'

PAUL TOURNIER
BORN 1898

Paul Tournier's father, a well-known Geneva preacher, died when Paul was only three months old. Six years later his mother died too. His lonely childhood, during which he was cared for by an aunt, gave him a lifelong concern for those who suffer psychologically. At the age of twelve he decided that he wanted to be a doctor. After World War I he worked with the Red Cross among ex-prisoners of war, and then began his career as a general practitioner in Geneva, where he stayed until his retirement.

In 1932 he encountered some members of a new religious movement, the Oxford Group. Their commitment to Jesus Christ and to each other brought him to a new experience of living faith. Gradually he became convinced that medicine which treated only physical and not spiritual ailments was inadequate. So he developed the idea of the 'medicine of the person', and wrote to all his patients explaining that from now on he would seek to help them through the insights of psychology and faith as well as through the usual types of medicine. At the same time he began to write about his experiences of holistic medicine in practice. His books have now sold millions of copies in sixteen languages. Written with a rare blend of human understanding and Christian wisdom, they appeal to people both from within and without the church.

Chastity is the most unpopular of the Christian virtues. There is no getting away from it: the old Christian rule is, 'Either marriage, with complete faithfulness to your partner, or else total abstinence.' Now this is so difficult and so contrary to our instincts, that obviously either Christianity is wrong or our sexual instinct, as it now is, has gone wrong. One or the other . . .

You can get a large audience together for a strip-tease act—that is, to watch a girl undress on the stage. Now suppose you came to a country where you could fill a theatre by simply bringing a covered plate on to the stage and then slowly lifting the cover so as to let everyone see, just before the lights went out, that it contained a mutton chop or a bit of bacon, would you not think that in that country something had gone wrong with the appetite for food? And would not anyone who had grown up in a different world think there was something equally queer about the state of the sex instinct among us?

FROM 'MERE CHRISTIANITY'

SERVING GOD IN EVERYTHING

For the fulfilment of his purpose God needs more than priests, bishops, pastors, and missionaries. He needs mechanics and chemists, gardeners and street sweepers, dressmakers and cooks, tradesmen, physicians, philosophers, judges, and shorthand typists . . . I do not serve God only in the brief moments during which I am taking part in a religious service, or reading the Bible, or saying my prayers, or talking about him in some book I am writing, or discussing the meaning of life with a patient or a friend. I serve him quite as much when I am giving a patient an injection, or lancing an abscess, or writing a prescription, or giving a piece of good advice. Or again, I serve him quite as much when I am reading the newspaper, travelling, laughing at a joke, or soldering a joint in an electric wire. I serve him by taking an interest in everything, because he is interested in everything, because he has created everything and has put me in his creation so that I may participate in it fully. 'It is a great mistake,' wrote Archbishop William Temple, 'to suppose that God is interested only, or even primarily, in religion.'

FROM 'THE ADVENTURE OF LIVING'

A RELIGIOUS EXPERIENCE

I have had a close friendship with a group of French pastors who conducted evangelistic missions with wholehearted zeal in various parishes. After one of these, they were received, in the late evening, by one of the notables of the parish. The latter was expressing his enthusiasm for the spiritual message they had brought. He added: 'As a matter of fact, I too have had a religious experience.' And turning to his wife, he said: 'Would you mind going up to the attic and getting it? You remember I wrote it out and framed it. It must be in the big chest at the far end. These gentlemen would be interested to see it.' A moment later the wife came back with the famous religious experience under her arm, but she had to beg pardon for producing it in such a condition, because the rats had been at it and had left it in a lamentable state!

FROM 'THE PERSON REBORN'

ALAN PATON
BORN 1903

The title of his award-winning novel, *Cry the Beloved
Country*, suggests Alan Paton's deep love for his native South
Africa, but also his sadness for a land which has been torn apart by
racial strife. A former teacher and reformatory principal, and
founder of the now banned Liberal Party of South Africa, Paton
has been a full-time writer since 1948. Christian faith and social
concern are inseparable in his works, both fiction and non-fiction.
He has a special commitment to the reform of criminal law.
Cry the Beloved Country shows, through the story of the
black Rev. Kumalo and his son Absalom who has killed a white
man in a robbery, how social order has been broken down by the
destruction of African tribal unity. But throughout the novel,
written in the poetic rhythms of the Bible, runs a note of
reconciliation and hope—as in this extract, where Kumalo, grieving
for his son, is consoled by the preaching of his friend Rev.
Msimangu at a home for the blind.

THE PREACHER AT THE HOME FOR THE BLIND

Msimangu opened the book, and read to
them first from the book. And Kumalo had
not known that his friend had such a voice.
For the voice was of gold, and the voice had
love for the words it was reading. The voice
shook and beat and trembled, not as the
voice of an old man shakes and beats and
trembles, nor as a leaf shakes and beats and
trembles, but as a deep bell when it is
struck. For it was not only a voice of gold,
but it was the voice of a man whose heart
was golden, reading from a book of golden
words. And the people were silent, and
Kumalo was silent, for when are three such

things found in one place together? . . . Msimangu was reading these words:

> And I will bring the blind by a way
>   that they knew not
> I will lead them in paths that they
>   have not known
> I will make darkness light before them
>   and crooked things straight
> These things I will do unto them
>   and not forsake them.

Yes, he speaks to me, there is no doubt of it. He says we are not forsaken. For while I wonder for what we live and struggle and die, for while I wonder what keeps us living and struggling, men are sent to minister to the blind, white men are sent to minister to the black blind . . . Yes, he speaks to me, in such quiet and such simple words. We are grateful for the saints, he says, who lift up the heart in the days of our distress. Would we do less? For do we less, there are no saints to lift up any heart. If Christ be Christ he says, true Lord of Heaven, true Lord of Men, what is there that we would not do no matter what our suffering may be?

I hear you, my brother. There is no word I do not hear . . .

The people sigh, and Kumalo sighs, as though this is a great word that has been spoken. And indeed this Msimangu is known as a preacher. It is good for the Government, they say in Johannesburg, that Msimangu preaches of a world not made by hands, for he touches people at the hearts, and sends them marching to heaven instead of to Pretoria . . .

Yet he is despised by some, for this golden voice that could raise a nation, speaks always thus. For this place of suffering, from which men might escape if some such voice could bind them all together, is for him no continuing city. They say he preaches of a world not made by hands, while in the streets about him men suffer and struggle and die. They ask what folly it is that can so seize upon a man, what folly is it that seizes upon so many of their people, making the hungry patient, the suffering content, the dying at peace? And how fools listen to him, silent, enrapt, sighing when he is done, feeding their empty bellies on his empty words.

Kumalo goes to him.

—Brother, I am recovered.

Msimangu's face lights up, but he talks humbly, there is no pride or false constraint.

—I have tried every way to touch you, he says, but I could not come near. So give thanks and be satisfied.

DIETRICH BONHOEFFER

1906–1945

In the summer of 1939, Bonhoeffer, a Lutheran pastor
and lecturer in theology, was on a lecture tour in America. Already
he was known as an enemy of the Nazi regime in his native
Germany. He had denounced Hitler on the radio in 1933, before he
came to power. He had spent two years in London urging the
German congregation there to join the battle against Nazism. And
in 1936 he had been banned by the Nazis from speaking, writing or
lecturing. He had also written two influential books—*The Cost of
Discipleship* and *Living Together*—and his reputation as a radical
Christian thinker was growing. If he stayed in America, he would
be safe and could pursue his studies. Instead he chose to return to
Germany, taking one of the last ships to sail before war broke out.
After four years of resistance work, he was finally
arrested for his part in an attempt to assassinate Hitler. On 9 April
1945—only a short time before the end of the war—he was hanged.
His *Letters and Papers from Prison*, published after his death, show
a man who thought deeply about what Christianity means in
the modern world, and who lived out his faith to the end with
unfailing courage.

A WORLD COME OF AGE

God is being increasingly pushed out of a
world that has come of age, out of the
spheres of our knowledge and life, and . . .
since Kant he has been relegated to a realm
beyond the world of experience. Theology
has on the one hand resisted this development with apologetics, and has taken up
arms—in vain—against Darwinism, etc.
On the other hand, it has accommodated
itself to the development by restricting
God to the so-called ultimate questions as a
deus ex machina; that means that he
becomes the answer to life's problems, and
the solution of its needs and conflicts. So if
anyone has no such difficulties, or if he
refuses to go into these things, to allow
others to pity him, then either he cannot
be open to God; or else he must be shown
that he is, in fact, deeply involved in such
problems, needs, and conflicts, without
admitting or knowing it. If that can be
done—and existentialist philosophy and
psychotherapy have worked out some
quite ingenious methods in that direction
—then this man can now be claimed for

God, and methodism can celebrate its triumph. But if he cannot be brought to see and admit that his happiness is really an evil, his health sickness, and his vigour despair, the theologian is at his wits' end. It's a case of having to do either with a hardened sinner of a particularly ugly type, or with a man of 'bourgeois complacency', and the one is as far from salvation as the other.

You see, that is the attitude I am contending against. When Jesus blessed sinners, they were real sinners, but Jesus did not make everyone a sinner first. He called them away from their sin, not into their sin. It is true that encounter with Jesus meant the reversal of all human values. So it was in the conversion of Paul, though in his case the encounter with Jesus preceded the realization of sin. It is true that Jesus cared about people on the fringe of human society, such as harlots and tax-collectors, but never about them alone, for he sought to care about man as such. Never did he question a man's health, vigour or happiness, regarded in themselves, or regard them as evil fruits; else why should he heal the sick and restore strength to the weak? Jesus claims for himself and the Kingdom of God the whole of human life in all its manifestations.

Of course I have to be interrupted just now! Let me just summarize briefly what I'm concerned about—the claim of a world that has come of age by Jesus Christ.

I can't write any more today, or else the letter will be kept here another week, and I don't want that to happen. So: To be continued!

———————FROM 'LETTERS AND PAPERS FROM PRISON'———————

———————CHEAP GRACE AND COSTLY GRACE———————

Cheap grace is the deadly enemy of our church. We are fighting today for costly grace. Cheap grace means grace sold on the market like cheapjack's wares. The sacraments, the forgiveness of sin, and the consolations of religion are thrown away at cut prices. Grace is represented as the church's inexhaustible treasury, from which she showers blessing with generous hands, without asking questions or fixing limits . . . Cheap grace is the preaching of forgiveness without requiring repentance, baptism without church discipline, Communion without confession, absolution without personal confession. Cheap grace is grace without discipleship, grace without the cross, grace without Jesus Christ, living and incarnate.

Costly grace is the treasure hidden in the field; for the sake of it a man will gladly go and sell all that he has. It is the pearl of great price to buy which the merchant will sell all his goods. It is the kingly rule of Christ, for whose sake a man will pluck out the eye which causes him to stumble, it is the call of Jesus Christ at which the disciple leaves his nets and follows him.

Costly grace is the gospel which must be *sought* again and again, the gift which must be *asked* for, the door at which a man must *knock*.

Such grace is *costly* because it calls us to follow, and it is grace because it calls us to follow *Jesus Christ*. It is costly because it costs a man his life, and it is grace because it gives a man the only true life. It is costly because it condemns sin, and grace because it justifies the sinner. Above all it is costly because it cost God the life of his Son: 'ye were bought at a price', and what has cost God much cannot be cheap for us.

———————FROM 'THE COST OF DISCIPLESHIP'———————

SIMONE WEIL

1909–1943

The daughter of an affluent Jewish doctor in Paris,
Simone Weil showed early intellectual brilliance, taking her
'baccalaureat' at only fifteen. Philosophy was her first love. But
along with this went a fierce concern for the underprivileged—even
as a small child she refused to wear warm socks because poor
children went without!
In 1936 she joined the International Brigade in the
Spanish Civil War and suffered burns in the fighting. While
convalescing in Portugal, she went to a cathedral service and
suddenly felt 'a presence more personal, more certain, more real
than that of a human being'. This was the first of many mystical
experiences of Christ. After World War II broke out she went to
Marseilles to do agricultural work (at the same time studying
Sanskrit and Greek and Hindu philosophy!). There she met Father
Perrin who became her spiritual director and to whom the passage
below was written. She was deeply attracted to the Catholic church
but felt unworthy to receive baptism. 'The bell which tolls to draw
others to church' was how she described herself.
Persuaded by her parents to leave France, she worked in
England for the Free French Government. Ill health, especially
severe headaches, had always troubled her, and now she was found
to have tuberculosis. But she refused to eat any more than the
amount her fellow French had in their rations. Her death was
largely due to starvation.

SOUGHT BY GOD

I may say that never at any moment in my life have I 'sought for God'. For this reason, which is probably too subjective, I do not like this expression and it strikes me as false. As soon as I reached adolescence, I saw the problem of God as a problem the data of which could not be obtained here below, and I decided that the only way of being sure not to reach a wrong solution, which seemed to me the greatest possible evil, was to leave it alone. So I left it alone. I neither affirmed nor denied anything . . . I knew quite well that my conception of life was Christian. That is why it never occurred to me that I could enter the Christian community. I had the idea that I was born inside. But to add dogma to this conception of life, without being forced to do so by indisputable evidence, would have

seemed to me like a lack of honesty . . . For it seemed to me certain, and I still think so today, that one can never wrestle enough with God if one does so out of pure regard for the truth. Christ likes us to prefer truth to him because, before being Christ, he is truth. If one turns aside from him to go toward the truth, one will not go far before falling into his arms . . .

Last summer, doing Greek with T____, I went through the Our Father word for word in Greek. We promised each other to learn it by heart. I do not think he ever did so, but some weeks later, as I was turning over the pages of the Gospel, I said to myself that since I had promised to do this thing and it was good, I ought to do it. I did it. The infinite sweetness of this Greek text so took hold of me that for several days I

could not stop myself from saying it over all the time . . .

Since that time I have made a practice of saying it through once each morning with absolute attention . . . The effect of this practice is extraordinary and surprises me every time, for, although I experience it each day, it exceeds my expectation at each repetition. At times the very first words tear my thoughts from my body and transport it to a place outside space where there is neither perspective nor point of view . . . At the same time, filling every part of this infinity of infinity, there is silence, a silence which is not an absence of sound but which is the object of a positive sensation, more positive than that of sound . . . Sometimes, also, during this recitation or at other moments, Christ is present with me in person, but his presence is infinitely more real, more moving, more clear than on that first occasion when he took possession of me . . .

I have told you that you are like a father and brother at the same time to me. But these words only express an analogy. Perhaps at bottom they only correspond to a feeling of affection, of gratitude and admiration. For as to the spiritual direction of my soul, I think that God himself has taken it in hand from the start and still looks after it.

FROM 'WAITING FOR GOD'

ANTHONY BLOOM
BORN 1914

The son of a Russian diplomat, Anthony Bloom spent
his early childhood in Persia. After the Russian revolution the
family travelled by horse-cart and barge across India and Europe
and eventually settled in Paris. But the return to security left
Anthony, then fourteen, strangely dissatisfied. He gave himself a
year to find the meaning of life. If he failed, he intended to commit
suicide. During this time, he heard a priest speak at a Russian
youth organization. What he heard repelled him so much that he
went home and read Mark's Gospel (chosen because it was the
shortest!) to see if it was true. 'Before I reached the third chapter I
suddenly became aware that on the other side of my desk there was
a presence. And the certainty that it was Christ has never left me.'

Supporting himself by teaching, and often studying all
night, he graduated in sciences from the Sorbonne. He spent World
War II partly as an army surgeon and partly in the Resistance.
After secretly taking monastic vows, in 1948 he was ordained. He
came to Britain (knowing no English!) to be chaplain to the
Fellowship of St Alban and St Sergius, an Anglican-Russian
Orthodox association. He is now Metropolitan of Sourozh
(equivalent to a Western archbishop). His books on prayer, written
with warm humour, open up the rich tradition of Orthodox
spirituality to a wide readership.

THE WORKSHOP SUPERVISOR

In 1938 a man died on Mount Athos. He
was a very simple man, a peasant from
Russia who came to Mount Athos when he
was in his twenties and stayed for about
fifty years . . . For a long time he was in
charge of the workshops of the monastery.
The workshops of the monastery were
manned by young Russian peasants who
used to come for one year, for two years, in
order to make some money, really farthing

added to farthing, in order to go back to
their villages with a few pounds, perhaps,
at the utmost to be able to start a family by
marrying, by building a hut and by buying
enough to start their crops.

One day other monks, who were in
charge of other workshops, said 'Father
Silouan, how is it that the people who work
in your workshops work so well while you
never supervise them, while we spend our

A monk working in the monastery on Mount Athos.

time looking after them and they try continuously to cheat us in their work?' Father Silouan said 'I don't know. I can only tell you what I do about it. When I come in the morning, I never come without having prayed for these people and I come with my heart filled with compassion and with love for them, and when I walk into the workshop I have tears in my soul for love of them. And then I give them the task they have to perform in the day and as long as they will work I will pray for them, so I go into my cell and I begin to pray about each of them individually. I take my stand before God and I say "O Lord, remember Nicholas. He is young, he is just twenty, he has left in his village his wife, who is even younger than he, and their first child. Can you imagine the misery there is there that he has had to leave them because they

could not survive on his work at home? Protect them in his absence. Shield them against every evil. Give him courage to struggle through this year and go back to the joy of a meeting, with enough money, but also enough courage, to face the difficulties."' And he said 'In the beginning I prayed with tears of compassion for Nicholas, for his young wife, for the little child, but as I was praying the sense of the divine presence began to grow on me and at a certain moment it grew so powerful that I lost sight of Nicholas, of his wife, his child, his needs, their village, and I could be aware only of God, and I was drawn by the sense of the divine presence deeper and deeper, until of a sudden, at the heart of this presence, I met the divine love holding Nicholas, his wife, and his child, and now it was with the love of God that I began to pray for them again, but again I was drawn into the deep and in the depths of this I again found the divine love. 'And so', he said, 'I spend my days, praying for each of them in turn, one after the other, and when the day is over I go, I say a few words to them, we pray together and they go to their rest. And I go back to fulfil my monastic office.'

―――――― FROM 'SCHOOL FOR PRAYER' ――――――

For centuries Mount Athos in Greece has been an important
centre of monasticism for the Orthodox church.

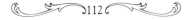

THOMAS MERTON
1915–1968

Like many others before him, starting with Augustine,
Merton is perhaps best known for his autobiography. *The Seven
Storey Mountain*, first published in 1948, describes vividly and with
wit his childhood as the son of an American artist in France, his
private education in England, his involvement with the Young
Communists while teaching English at Columbia University and
his work in a Harlem settlement. But it is above all an account of
the spiritual journey which took him from atheism to Catholicism
and eventually into the silence of the Trappist monastery of
Gethsemani, Kentucky. He lived there in increasing seclusion,
spending his last years in a cabin in the woods from which he
emerged only for his one meal a day and to fetch fresh water. Yet
his writings—spiritual, political and poetic—spoke to millions of
how the monastic commitment can be a sign of God's presence in
the world today. He was particularly interested in what Christians
can learn from Eastern spirituality. It was during a visit to
Bangkok, Thailand, for a conference on Christianity and Buddhism
that he met his tragic death from electrocution.

──────── CHRISTMAS IN THE MONASTERY ────────

Christ always seeks the straw of the most
desolate cribs to make his Bethlehem. In all
the other Christmases of my life, I had got
a lot of presents and a big dinner. This
Christmas I was to get no presents, and not
much of a dinner; but I would have,

indeed, Christ himself, God, the Saviour of
the world.

You who live in the world: let me tell
you that there is no comparing these two
kinds of Christmas.

What an atmosphere of expectation

and joy there is in a Cistercian monastery when the monks get up, not at two in the morning, but at nine in the evening. They have gone to bed at five. Now, at this unaccustomed hour, when the winter night has not yet begun to get that paralysing desolate coldness of the small hours, the church is full of unaccustomed lights. There is the crib, all lit up with a soft glow, and in the high darkness of the sanctuary the forest of cedar branches that has grown up around the altar sparkles with tinsel here and there.

It is then that the night office begins at once with a solemn and stately invitatory that nevertheless rocks the church with cadences of superlative joy; from then on it is as though the angels themselves were singing their *Gloria in Excelsis* and showering upon the earth from the near stars, the stars that seem to have become close and warm, their messages and promises of peace, peace! Peace on earth to men of good will. As the Midnight Mass begins, the whole place glows with happiness, and after that it is indescribable, building up to the climax of unworldly interior peace at Communion.

It is good that somewhere in the world there are men who realize that Christ is born. There were only a few shepherds at the first Bethlehem, and it is the same now. The ox and the ass understood more of the first Christmas than the high priests in Jerusalem. And it is the same today.

—————————FROM 'THE SEVEN STOREY MOUNTAIN'—————————

Woodland in Kentucky.

FACING DEATH WITHOUT FAITH

I lay back in bed and closed my eyes and thought, 'I have blood poisoning.'

Blood poisoning.

The room was very quiet. It was rather dark, too. And as I lay in bed, in my weariness and pain and disgust, I felt for a moment the shadow of another visitor pass into the room.

It was death, that came to stand by my bed.

I kept my eyes closed, more out of apathy than anything else. But anyway, there was no need to open one's eyes to see the visitor, to see death. Death is someone you see very clearly with eyes in the centre of your heart: eyes that see not by reacting to light, but by reacting to a kind of chill from within the marrow of your own life.

And, with those eyes, those interior eyes, open upon that coldness I lay half asleep and looked at the visitor, death.

What did I think? All I remember was that I was filled with a deep and tremendous apathy. I felt so sick and disgusted that I did not very much care whether I died or lived. Perhaps death did not come very close to me, or give me a good look at the nearness of his coldness and darkness, or I would have been more afraid.

But at any rate, I lay there in a kind of torpor and said: 'Come on, I don't care.' And then I fell asleep . . .

Religious people, those who have faith and love God and realize what life is and what death means, and know what it is to have an immortal soul, do not understand how it is with the ones who have no faith, and who have already thrown away their souls. They find it hard to conceive that anyone could enter into the presence of death without some kind of compunction. But they should realize that millions of men die the way I was then prepared to die, the way I might then have died.

FROM THE FIRST DRAFT OF 'THE SEVEN STOREY MOUNTAIN'

ALEXANDER SOLZHENITSYN

BORN 1918

'One word of truth outweighs the whole world.' On this Russian proverb Solzhenitsyn based his acceptance speech when he was awarded the Nobel Prize for Literature in 1970. He had been writing on and off from the age of ten, but he took his degree in mathematics and physics, not literature, in order to study near to his widowed mother. 'Mathematics,' he later said, 'unfailingly came to my aid in all the difficult periods of my life.'

The difficult periods started when in 1945 he was arrested by the Soviet authorities for remarks he had made about Stalin. He spent eight years in labour camps, followed by a 'permanent exile' (from which he was later released). This experience inspired his first novel, *One Day in the Life of Ivan Denisovich*, which was an outstanding success in the West and was later filmed. In 1969, however, he was expelled from the Writers' Union as a result of a letter protesting against censorship. Acclamation in the West only increased Soviet suspicion of him, and in 1974 he was expelled from the USSR after a protest to the Soviet leadership. He now lives in the USA with his second wife and three sons.

Solzhenitsyn has gradually come to see the Christian faith as 'the only force capable of undertaking the spiritual healing of Russia'. But his faith leads him to criticize Western materialism just as strongly as he does the Soviet system. His Nobel lecture, which he was unable to deliver in person, has been described as 'a magnificent and moving statement of the artist's role as the conscience of mankind'.

THE GIFT OF ART

As the savage, confronted with a strange object, asks himself, 'Was it cast up by the ocean? Has it been long buried in the sand? Did it fall from the sky?'—an intricately curved object, reflecting the light now dimly, now with flashing brilliance—turns it this way and that in bewilderment, twists it, tries to adapt it to some purpose, seeks to find some lowly acceptable use for it, never suspecting its higher purpose, so we too, holding Art in our hands, conceitedly deem ourselves its masters. We boldly direct, renew, reform and proclaim it, sell it for money, flatter the powerful with it, employ it sometimes for entertainment—even for popular songs and nightclub revues; sometimes we use it as a stop-gap or a weapon for transitory political and limited social needs. But Art is not sullied by our efforts; it loses nothing of its lineage, but every time and however applied it grants us a share of its own secret, inner light . . .

One artist imagines himself to be the creator of an independent spiritual world, burdens himself with the act of creating

Solzhenitsyn (left) in conversation with a friend.

and peopling this world, accepts complete responsibility for it—but he breaks down, because no mortal genius is capable of withstanding such a burden just as, in a more general sense man, who has declared himself to be the centre of existence, has been unable to create a balanced spiritual system. And if he is overwhelmed by failure, he lays the blame on the eternal disharmony of the world, on the complexity of the distraught contemporary soul, or on the lack of comprehension of the public.

Another artist knows there is a higher power over him and will work joyfully as a small apprentice under God's heaven, although his responsibility for everything he paints and draws, and for the souls who apprehend it, is greater. But on the other hand this world was not created by him, is not ruled by him, there are no doubts about its fundamental principles; this artist has only the gift of perceiving more acutely than others the harmony of the world and the beauty and ugliness of man's contribution to it, and the gift of acutely conveying this to others. In failure and even in the lowest depths of existence—in destitution, in prison, in sickness—the consciousness of this steadfast harmony cannot forsake him.

However the whole irrationality of Art, its dazzling convolutions, its unpredictable discoveries, its shattering influence on people are too magical to be plumbed by an artist's philosophy or scheme of things or by the labour of his unworthy hands . . .

Not everything has a name. Some things lead us into a realm beyond words. Art thaws even the frozen, darkened soul, opening it to lofty spiritual experience. Through Art we are sometimes sent—indistinctly, briefly—revelations not to be achieved by rational thought.

It is like that small mirror in the fairy tales—you glance in it and what you see is not yourself; for an instant you glimpse the Inaccessible, where no horse or magic carpet can take you. And the soul cries out for it . . .

——— FROM 'ONE WORD OF TRUTH' ———

Madeleine L'Engle
BORN 1919

Born in New York, Madeleine L'Engle received part of her education in Europe where her father worked as a foreign correspondent. After studying English at universities in America, she worked in the theatre, where she met her actor husband, and then began to teach, lecture and write. Five novels for adults were published, and then suddenly her inspiration dried up. For ten years she wrote nothing; her husband left the theatre and together they ran their local general store. Then she began to write again— for children. Her science fiction fantasy with a Christian message, *A Wrinkle in Time*, took a while to find a publisher. But then in 1962 it won the Newbery Medal, the highest honour for children's writing in America, and several other awards. Not since C. S. Lewis' 'Narnia' books has spiritual truth been so effectively presented to children. The story of the Murry family's struggle against the evil power of IT, aided by the lovable 'guardian angels' Mrs Who, Mrs Whatsit and Mrs Which, has captivated thousands of adults too.

BEING DIFFERENT

Charles continued his lecture. 'On Camazotz we are all happy because we are all alike. Differences create problems. You know that, don't you, dear sister?'

'No,' Meg said.

'Oh, yes, you do. You've seen at home how true it is. You know that's the reason you're not happy at school. Because you're different.'

'But I'm different, and I'm happy,' Calvin said.

'But you pretend that you *aren't* different.'

'I'm different, and I like being different,' Calvin's voice was unnaturally loud.

'Maybe I don't like being different,' Meg said, 'but I don't want to be like everybody else, either.'

. . . Charles Wallace's strange, monotonous voice ground against her ears. 'Meg, you're supposed to have *some* mind. Why do you think we have wars at home? Why do you think people get confused and unhappy? Because they all live their own, separate, individual lives. I've been trying to explain to you in the simplest possible way that on Camazotz individuals have been done away with. Camazotz is ONE mind. It's IT. And that's why everybody is happy and efficient . . . Meg shook her head violently, 'No!' she shouted. 'I know our world isn't perfect, Charles, but it's better than this. This isn't the only alternative! It can't be!'

'Nobody suffers here,' Charles intoned. 'Nobody is ever unhappy.'

'But nobody's happy, either,' Meg said earnestly. 'Maybe if you aren't unhappy sometimes you don't know how to be happy. Calvin, I want to go home.'

'We can't leave Charles,' Calvin told her, 'and we can't go before we've found your father. You know that. But you're right, Meg, and Mrs Which is right. This is Evil.'

MARTIN LUTHER KING JNR

1928–1968

In 1955 King, the son and grandson of Baptist ministers,
was serving as pastor of a Baptist church in Montgomery, Alabama,
when a black woman was arrested for sitting in the 'whites only'
section of a segregated bus. King found himself leading the resulting
bus boycott, the success of which is described below. From then on
he was a key figure in the Civil Rights movement, leading
the famous 1963 march on Washington which brought about two
major Civil Rights Acts, and the campaign to encourage blacks to
register as voters. In 1964 he was awarded the Nobel Peace Prize.
King's inspiration was the message of Jesus, and his
method was the non-violent resistance of Gandhi. 'We shall match
your capacity to inflict suffering with our capacity to endure
suffering', he said to his opponents. 'Do to us what you will and we
shall continue to love you . . .' His approach drew attacks both
from white conservatives and black revolutionaries; and in 1968 he
paid for it with his life, shot down by a white gunman.

LOVE CAN
CONQUER HATE

The oceans of history are made turbulent
by the ever-rising tides of revenge. Man has
never risen above the injunction of the lex
talionis: 'Life for life, eye for eye, tooth for
tooth, hand for hand, foot for foot.' In spite
of the fact that the law of revenge solves no
social problems, men continue to follow its
disastrous leading. History is cluttered with
the wreckage of nations and individuals
that pursued this self-defeating path.

Jesus eloquently affirmed from the cross
a higher law. He knew that the old eye-for-
an-eye philosophy would leave everyone
blind. He did not seek to overcome evil
with evil. He overcame evil with good.
Although crucified by hate, he responded
with aggressive love.

What a magnificent lesson! Generations
will rise and fall; men will continue to
worship the god of revenge and bow before
the altar of retaliation; but ever and again
this noble lesson of Calvary will be a
nagging reminder that only goodness can
drive out evil and only love can conquer
hate.

FROM 'STRENGTH TO LOVE'

At the beginning of the bus boycott in Montgomery, Alabama, we set up a voluntary car pool to get the people to and from their jobs. For eleven long months our car pool functioned extraordinarily well. Then Mayor Gayle introduced a resolution instructing the city's legal department to file such proceedings as it might deem proper to stop the operation of the car pool or any transportation system growing out of the bus boycott. A hearing was set for Tuesday, November 13, 1956.

At our regular weekly mass meeting, scheduled the night before the hearing, I had the responsibility of warning the people that the car pool would probably be enjoined. I knew that they had willingly suffered for nearly twelve months, but could we now ask them to walk back and forth to their jobs? And if not, would we be forced to admit that the protest had failed? For the first time I almost shrank from appearing before them.

When the evening came, I mustered sufficient courage to tell them the truth. I tried, however, to conclude on a note of hope. 'We have moved all of these months,' I said, 'in the daring faith that God is with us in our struggle. The many experiences of days gone by have vindicated that faith in a marvellous way. Tonight we must believe that a way will be made out of no way.' Yet I could feel the cold breeze of pessimism pass over the audience. The night was darker than a thousand midnights. The light of hope was about to fade and the lamp of faith to flicker.

A few hours later, before Judge Carter, the city argued that we were operating a 'private enterprise' without a franchise. Our lawyers argued brilliantly that the car pool was a voluntary 'share-a-ride' plan provided without profit as a service by Negro churches. It became obvious that Judge Carter would rule in favour of the city.

At noon, during a brief recess, I noticed an unusual commotion in the courtroom. Mayor Gayle was called to the back room. Several reporters moved excitedly in and out of the room. Momentarily a reporter came to the table where, as chief defendant, I sat with the lawyers. 'Here is the decision that you have been waiting for,' he said. 'Read this release.'

In anxiety and hope, I read these words: 'The United States Supreme Court today unanimously ruled bus segregation unconstitutional in Montgomery, Alabama.' My heart throbbed with an inexpressible joy. The darkest hour of our struggle had become the first hour of victory.

FROM 'STRENGTH TO LOVE'

Index of Authors

Acknowledgements

The following material is copyright and is included by kind permission of the copyright holders

'The Fellowship of the Spirit' from *The Didache* reprinted by permission of Penguin Books Ltd from *Early Christian Writings* by Maxwell Stanniforth.

Eusebius, 'The Death of Polycarp, Bishop of Smyrna' reprinted by permission of Penguin Books Ltd from *Early Christian Writings* by Maxwell Stanniforth.

'Augustine's Conversion' and 'Late Have I Loved' reprinted by permission of Penguin Books Ltd from *The Confessions of Augustine* translated by R. S. Pine-Coffin.

'Mary Needs Martha' taken from Thomas Merton, *The Wisdom of the Desert*. Copyright © 1960 by the Abbey of Gethsemani Inc. Reprinted by permission of New Directions Publishing Corporation.

Extracts from Benedict's *Rule* taken from *Households of God* translated by David Parry, published and copyright © 1980 by Darton, Longman and Todd Ltd, London, and is used by permission of the publishers.

Anselm, 'The Reality of God' reprinted by permission of Penguin Books Ltd from *Prayers and Meditations of St Anselm* translated by Benedicta Ward.

Bernard of Clairvaux, 'The Poverty of Riches' reprinted by permission of A. R. Mowbray and Co. Ltd from *On the Love of God*, copyright © 1961.

Francis of Assisi, 'Treasure' reprinted by permission of Penguin Books Ltd from *The Little Flowers of St Francis* translated by Leo Sherley-Price; 'The Way to Humility' reprinted by permission of A. R. Mowbray and Co. Ltd from *St Francis of Assisi: His Life and Writings* translated by Leo Sherley-Price, copyright © 1959.

Thomas Aquinas, 'New Words for Old Truths' and 'Ways of Proving God' reprinted by permission of Hodder and Stoughton Ltd from *An Aquinas Reader* edited by Mary T. Clarke. For USA: reprinted by permission of Doubleday and Co. Inc. from *An Aquinas Reader* edited by Mary T. Clarke.

Meister Eckhart, 'Emptying the Cask' reprinted by permission of The Missionary Society of St Paul the Apostle in the State of New York from *Meister Eckhart: The Sermons, Commentaries, Treatises and Defense* copyright © 1981.

Julian of Norwich, 'All That Is Made' and 'The Meaning of the Visions' reprinted by permission of Penguin Books Ltd from *Revelations of Divine Love*.

Extract from *The Cloud of Unknowing* reprinted by permission of Penguin Books Ltd from *The Cloud of Unknowing* translated by Clifton Wolters.

Catherine of Siena, 'The Bridge' reprinted by permission of William Collins Sons and Co. Ltd from *I, Catherine* translated by Kenelm Foster, 1980.

William Langland, 'A Professional Pilgrim' reprinted by permission of Penguin Books Ltd from *Piers Ploughman* translated by J. F. Goodridge.

Thomas à Kempis, extracts reprinted by permission of Penguin Books Ltd from *The Imitation of Christ* translated by Leo Sherley-Price.

Erasmus, 'The Bible for Everyone' from *Christian Humanism and the Reformation* translated by John C. Olin, Harper and Row, 1965; 'Fools for Christ' from *The Essential Erasmus* edited by John Dolan, New English Library, 1964.

Thomas More, 'The Utopian's Attitude to Wealth' reprinted by permission of Penguin Books Ltd from *Utopia* edited by Paul Turner.

Martin Luther, extracts reprinted by permission of Edward Arnold from *Martin Luther* edited by Rupp and Drewry, Documents of Modern History series.

John Calvin, 'Only Through Christ' and 'The Role of the Government' reprinted by permission of SCM Press from *Institutes of the Christian Religion* (2 volumes), Library of Christian Classics, 1961. For USA: extracts from *Calvin: Institutes of the Christian Religion*, edited by John T. McNeill; translated by Ford Lewis Battles (Volume XX: The Library of Christian Classics). Copyright © MCMLX W. L. Jenkins. Used by permission of The Westminster Press, Philadelphia, PA.

John of the Cross, 'From Milk to Solid Food' reprinted by permission of Burns and Oates Ltd from *The Complete Works of John of the Cross* edited by E. Allison Peers.

Blaise Pascal, extracts reprinted by permission of J. M. Dent and Sons Ltd from *Pensées* translated by W. F. Trotter, Everyman's Library, 1941.

Søren Kierkegaard, 'Complaining to God' reprinted by permission of the University of Notre Dame Press, from *Repetitions* translated by Colette.

Karl Barth, 'Saved By Grace' reprinted by permission of The Epworth Press from *Modern Theology* edited by E. J. Tinsley.

C. S. Lewis, extracts from *The Voyage of the Dawn Treader*, *Mere Christianity*, *The Screwtape Letters* and *The Silver Chair* reprinted by permission of William Collins Sons and Co. Ltd.

Paul Tournier, 'A Religious Experience' reprinted by permission of SCM Press from *The Person Reborn*, 1967; 'Serving God in Everything' reprinted by permission of SCM Press from *The Adventure of Living*, 1960.

Alan Paton, 'The Preacher at the Home for the Blind' reprinted by permission of Jonathan Cape Ltd from *Cry, The Beloved Country*. For USA: Alan Paton, specified excerpt from *Cry, The Beloved Country*. Copyright © 1948 Alan Paton. Copyright renewed 1976 Alan Paton. Reprinted with permission of Charles Scribner's Sons.

Dietrich Bonhoeffer, 'A World Come Of Age', reprinted by permission of SCM Press from *Letters and Papers from Prison*, edited by Eberhard Bethge, copyright © 1953, 1967, 1971; 'Cheap Grace and Costly Grace' reprinted by permission of SCM Press from *The Cost of Discipleship*, 1959.

Simone Weil, 'Sought By God' from *Waiting for God* translated by Emma Craufurd, Harper and Row, 1973.

Anthony Bloom, 'The Workshop Supervisor' taken from *School For Prayer* by Anthony Bloom, published and copyright © 1970 by Darton, Longman and Todd Ltd, London, and is used by permission of the publishers.

Thomas Merton, 'Facing Death Without Faith' from *A Thomas Merton Reader*. Copyright by the Abbey of Gethsemani, Inc. Reprinted by permission of New Directions Publishing Corporation.

Medeleine L'Engle, 'Being Different' reprinted by permission of Penguin Books Ltd from *A Wrinkle in Time*.

Martin Luther King Jnr, 'Victory Against Racism' and 'Love Can Conquer Hate' reprinted by permission of the Estate of the Late Dr Martin Luther King, Jnr, from *Strength to Love*, copyright © 1963 by Martin Luther King, Jnr.

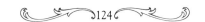

Credits

Photographs and illustrations:

BBC Hulton Picture Library, pages 63, 64, 76, 91, 100; British
Library, page 19; Photographie Bulloz, page 61; Camerapix-
Hutchinson, pages 114–15; J. Allan Cash Photolibrary, pages 45,
76, 77; Mary Evans Picture Library, pages 30, 40, 42, 52, 68, 73,
85, 86–87; Sonia Halliday Photographs/Bibliotheque Nationale
page 16, FHC Birch pages 25, 54, Sonia Halliday pages 10, 15, 17,
28, 38 (both), 41, 44, 101, 113, Jane Taylor pages 24, 104–105;
Michael Holford, page 27; Tony Lane, pages 51, 52, 68 (inset), 80;
Lion Publishing, pages 12, 48 (both), 65; Mansell Collection,
pages 14, 20, 22, 34, 43, 46, 49, 55, 59, 67, 69, 79, 82;
Picturepoint, page 111; The Salvation Army, pages 92–93; S and
G Press Agency, pages 117, 121; SCM Press, page 106;
Spurgeon's College, page 97 (both); Werner Neumeister DGPh,
page 99; ZEFA, pages 33, 37, 112 and cover.
The illustration on page 62 is from *Pascal Par Lui-meme* by Albert Beguin.
The illustration on page 89 is by Maud Humphreys and is taken
from *The Light Princess and Other Fairy Tales* by George MacDonald.

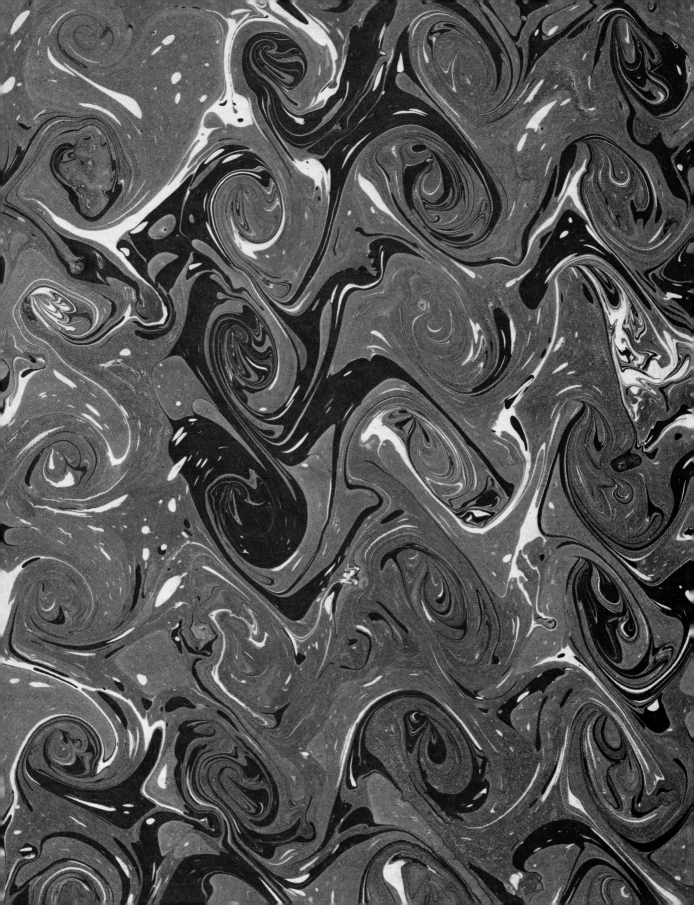